BERYL M. MA

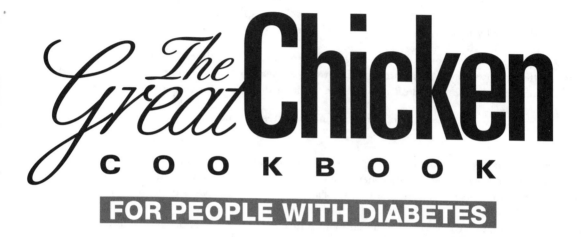

The Great Chicken COOKBOOK

FOR PEOPLE WITH DIABETES

▲® American Diabetes Association®

Book Acquisitions	Robert J. Anthony
Editor	Sherrye Landrum
Production Director	Carolyn R. Segree
Production Coordinator	Peggy M. Rote
Composition	Harlowe Typography, Inc.
Text and Cover Design	Wickham & Associates, Inc.

Printed in the United States of America

1 3 5 7 9 10 8 6 4 2

The suggestions and information contained in this publication are generally consistent with the *Clinical Practice Recommendations* and other policies of the American Diabetes Association, but they do not represent the policy or position of the Association or any of its boards or committees. Reasonable steps have been taken to ensure the accuracy of the information presented. However, the American Diabetes Association cannot ensure the safety or efficacy of any product or service described in this publication. Individuals are advised to consult a physician or other appropriate health care professional before undertaking any diet or exercise program or taking any medication referred to in this publication. Professionals must use and apply their own professional judgment, experience, and training and should not rely solely on the information contained in this publication before prescribing any diet, exercise, or medication. The American Diabetes Association—its officers, directors, employees, volunteers, and members—assumes no responsibility or liability for personal or other injury, loss, or damage that may result from the suggestions or information in this publication.

ADA titles may be purchased for business or promotional use or for special sales. For information, please write to: Lee M. Romano, Special Sales & Promotions, at the address below.

American Diabetes Association
1660 Duke Street
Alexandria, Virginia 22314

Library of Congress Cataloging-in-Publication Data

Marton, Beryl M.
    The great chicken cookbook for people with diabetes/by Beryl M. Marton.
        p.   cm.
    ISBN 1–58040–022–1 (pbk.)
    1.   Diabetes—Diet therapy—Recipes. 2. Cookery (Chicken)
    I.   Title.
    RC662.M357   1999
    641.5'6314—dc21

        98–54450
        CIP

Contents

A Note about Food Labels

Many food labels in the grocery store use terms that can be confusing. To help you shop and eat better, here is a list of the common terms as defined by the Food and Drug Administration.

Sugar

Sugar Free: Less than 0.5 grams of sugar per serving.

No Added Sugar, Without Added Sugar, No Sugar Added: This does not mean the same as "sugar free." A label bearing these words means that no sugars were added during processing, or that processing does not increase the sugar content above the amount the ingredients naturally contain. Consult the nutrition information panel to see the total amount of sugar in this product.

Reduced Sugar: At least 25% less sugar per serving than the regular product.

Calories

Calorie Free: Fewer than 5 calories per serving.

Low Calorie: 40 calories or less per serving. (If servings are smaller than 30 grams, or smaller than 2 tablespoons, this means 40 calories or less per 50 grams of food.)

Reduced Calorie, Fewer Calories: At least 25% fewer calories per serving than the regular product.

Fat

Fat Free, Nonfat: Less than 0.5 grams of fat per serving.

Low Fat: 3 grams or less of fat per serving. (If servings are smaller than 30 grams, or smaller than 2 tablespoons, this means 3 grams or less of fat per 50 grams of food.)

The Great Chicken Cookbook for People with Diabetes

Reduced Fat, Less Fat: At least 25% less of fat per serving than the regular product.

Cholesterol
Cholesterol Free: Less than 2 milligrams of cholesterol, and 2 grams or less of saturated fat per serving.

Low Cholesterol: 20 milligrams or less of cholesterol, and 2 grams or less of saturated fat per serving.

Reduced Cholesterol, Less Cholesterol: At least 25% less cholesterol, and 2 grams or less of saturated fat per serving than the regular product.

Sodium
Sodium Free: Less than 5 milligrams of sodium per serving.

Low Sodium: 140 milligrams or less of sodium per serving.

Very Low Sodium: 35 milligrams or less of sodium per serving.

Reduced Sodium, Less Sodium: At least 25% less sodium per serving than the regular product.

Light or Lite Foods
Foods that are labeled "Light" or "Lite" are usually either lower in fat or lower in calories than the regular product. Some products may also be lower in sodium. Check the nutrition information label on the back of the product to make sure.

Meat and Poultry
Lean: Less than 10 grams of fat, 4.5 grams or less of saturated fat, and less than 95 milligrams of cholesterol per serving and per 100 grams.

Extra Lean: Less than 5 grams of fat, less than 2 grams of saturated fat, and less than 95 milligrams of cholesterol per serving and per 100 grams.

*I*ntroduction

The Great Chicken Cookbook for People with Diabetes is a cookbook for all people who choose to eat healthfully. In these recipes, cholesterol is kept within recommended daily amounts for people with heart problems—a condition that people with diabetes are at greater risk of developing. The fat content of every recipe is as low as it can be and still taste good. Each recipe has been tested both with and without added salt. There is some controversy, currently, about how salt affects blood pressure, so use your best judgment along with your doctor's recommendations. At any rate, all the recipes are healthy—very healthy—and can be used in any meal plan. If everyone would count carbohydrates or follow the exchange system used by people with diabetes, fewer people would have problems with obesity. Naturally, regular exercise is the other half of any successful health plan.

Chicken is one of the best sources of protein. Its calorie count is low when all fat and skin are removed. It is one of the most popular foods available—more chicken is sold than any other meat. Most households purchase it weekly for at least one or two meals, which is the phenomenon that led me to write this cookbook. Chicken lends itself to many different methods of preparation, as you see in the fifteen chapters in this book.

Proper Technique

When I was a young woman, salmonella was unheard of. Today it is far too common. Wash all chicken thoroughly both inside and out before you cook it. Also wash the counters and utensils that you use thoroughly with soap and water. I wash the chicken in the sink under cold running water. I remove all the skin and fat and discard it, placing the chicken on paper towels to pat dry. Then I scrub the sink.

I find certain utensils and kitchen appliances are indispensable. Food processors can save you hours of preparation time. Blenders puree beautifully and mix liquids admirably, but they do not chop well. The food processor can do all these procedures and more. Pepper mills produce ground pepper that is so far superior to packaged pepper that once you use it, you will never go back.

There are certain facts you should know about cooking poultry that make it much easier to get a good result. Breast meat, for instance, cooks much faster than dark meat. If cooked more than 20 minutes, it becomes stringy and dry. Dark meat, however, takes longer. It should be cooked at least 30–35 minutes. Overcooking poultry is not desirable, but undercooking it is not healthy. Follow the cooking instructions in a given recipe carefully, and the results should be great.

I have used olive and canola oils in those recipes calling for oil. These two monounsaturated oils are considered the healthiest. I have also used nonfat cooking spray throughout the book and think a quick lesson in its proper use might be appropriate. Heat a nonstick skillet or saucepan. Liberally spray it with nonfat cooking spray. Add the food to be sautéed or browned. Over medium-low heat, cook, stirring constantly, until of desired doneness. Spray again during this process as often as needed to prevent scorching. When browning chicken or other meat, use the same method, and turn the poultry or meat often, re-spraying as needed. Another excellent way to brown chicken parts is to run them under the broiler for a few minutes to brown on each side.

Sauce making still frightens some people, and a few tips might help. Always remember that the liquid used and the cooked fat and flour mixture (roux) must be the same temperature. Cook

The Great Chicken Cookbook for People with Diabetes

the roux for 2–3 minutes. Take it off the heat, and add the boiling liquid all at once, beating vigorously with a wire whisk to prevent lumping. Return the pan to the stove and cook, stirring, until the sauce is thickened and smooth. You should have a fool-proof sauce. When you want to stir flour into a cold liquid and use it for thickening a sauce or gravy, the quick-mixing flours available today work wonders, eliminating lumps entirely. When you use cornstarch as a thickener, remember to dissolve the cornstarch in cold water, stock, or wine before adding it to the sauce.

Ingredients

A wide variety of vegetables, fruits, condiments, herbs, and spices are used in the recipes. Fruits from the tropics, exotic vegetables, and many fresh herbs can be found in markets throughout the United States and Canada. Packages of tiny baby carrots have become a staple, as are red, yellow, purple, and the tried and true green bell peppers. Hot peppers of every variety have their own space in the produce section, honoring the Latin American influence on the American table.

I have tried to use only those ingredients that are readily available in supermarkets all over the United States. I live in Maine, an area not noted for its sophistication—only its beauty. I have been able to find every ingredient called for in the recipes in this book. I have enjoyed writing it and testing each recipe. Believe it or not, chicken is still one of my favorite foods. Nothing is more satisfying than a good chicken dinner. Couple all that succulence with the "healthy" benefits, and I feel that this has truly been a labor of love.

Baked Chicken Dishes

This chapter covers all chicken dishes that require finishing in the oven using dry heat. Pies, tarts, quiche, and crepes fall into this category.

The crusts and toppings in the deep-dish pies in this section add to the fat content in the nutritional facts accompanying these recipes. If you want to, you can prepare these recipes without a crust or topping.

Plain Crust

Serves 8   Serving Size: 1/8 recipe

> 1 cup flour
> 1/4 tsp salt (optional)
> 1/3 cup shortening
> 3 Tbsp ice water

1. Place flour and salt in the jar of a food processor (or a mixing bowl). Add shortening and blend (or cut in with knives or pastry cutter) until crumbly. Add water 1 Tbsp at a time. Blend until the pastry leaves the side of the jar or mixing bowl.

2. Remove from jar, flatten into a 1 × 5-inch thick disc. Refrigerate 15 minutes. Roll into a circle to fit an 8- or 9-inch pie plate. Drape over plate, leaving a 2-inch overhang. Fold overhang up over pie plate edges. Crimp or flute attractively.

To prebake: Prick bottom of pie shell with a fork. Place a piece of aluminum foil on top of the crust, pressing it to the shape of the pie plate. Fill with dried beans. Place in a preheated 425° oven and bake 10 minutes. Cool. Remove foil and beans. Keep beans for baking crusts in the future. Makes 1 piecrust.

Exchanges
1/2 Starch
1 1/2 Fat

Calories 131
  Calories from Fat . . 77
Total Fat . . . . 8 g
  Saturated Fat . . . . . . 2 g
Cholesterol . . . . 0 mg
Sodium . . . . 67 mg
  W/o added salt . . . . . 1 mg
Carbohydrate . . . . . . 12 g
  Dietary Fiber . . . . . . 0 g
  Sugars . . . . 0 g
Protein . . . . 2 g

Potato Crust

Serves 8   Serving Size: 1/8 recipe

    1   lb baking potatoes
    1   oz egg substitute
    1   tsp salt (optional)
        Freshly ground pepper to taste
  1/2   tsp ground nutmeg
        Nonfat cooking spray

1. Scrub potatoes and prick with a fork. Bake in a preheated 425° oven for 1 hour.

2. Cut in half and scrape out insides. Mash well. Add remaining ingredients.

3. Spray a 9-inch pie plate with cooking spray. Press potato mixture into the bottom and up the sides, using a wet spoon. Prick bottom with a fork and place in a preheated 425° oven, and bake 12 minutes. Cool.

Exchanges
1 Starch

Calories 56
  Calories from Fat . . . 2
Total Fat . . . . 0 g
  Saturated Fat . . . . . . 0 g
Cholesterol . . . . 0 mg
Sodium . . . . 276 mg
  W/o added salt . . . . . 9 mg
Carbohydrate . . . . . . 12 g
  Dietary Fiber . . . . . . 1 g
  Sugars . . . . 1 g
Protein . . . . 1 g

Sweet Potato Crust

Serves 8   Serving Size: 1/8 recipe

  1 cup sifted flour
  1 tsp baking powder
1/2 tsp salt (optional)
1/2 tsp nutmeg
  1 cup cold mashed sweet potatoes
1/3 cup melted shortening
  1 egg, beaten

1. Sift flour with baking powder, salt, and nutmeg.

2. Blend in sweet potatoes, shortening, and egg.

3. Flatten into a 5 × 1-inch ring. Chill. Roll out to desired size.

Exchanges
1 Starch
1 1/2 Fat

Calories 184
  Calories from Fat . . 81
Total Fat . . . . 9 g
  Saturated Fat . . . . . . 2 g
Cholesterol . . . . 22 mg
Sodium . . . . 148 mg
  W/o added salt . . . . 14 mg
Carbohydrate . . . . . . 22 g
  Dietary Fiber . . . . . . 2 g
  Sugars . . . . 2 g
Protein . . . . 3 g

Cornmeal Crust

Serves 8   Serving Size: 1/8 recipe

1/4	cup cornmeal
1 1/2	cup flour
1	tsp salt (optional)
2/3	cup shortening
6	Tbsp ice water

1. Place cornmeal and flour in the jar of a food processor. Add salt and shortening. Blend until crumbly. Add water, 1 Tbsp at a time, through the tube, while machine is running, until dough leaves the side of the jar.

2. Form into a disc and refrigerate 15 minutes. Flour the rolling-out surface. Place disc on this surface and roll out to fit a pie shell or top of a casserole with a 2-inch overhang. Follow recipe instructions.

Exchanges
1 Starch
3 Fat

Calories	250
Calories from Fat	. 153
Total Fat	17 g
Saturated Fat	5 g
Cholesterol	0 mg
Sodium	267 mg
W/o added salt	1 mg
Carbohydrate	21 g
Dietary Fiber	1 g
Sugars	0 g
Protein	3 g

Rice Crust

Sushi rice is the best for this crust because of its stickiness, however, if it is not available, any short-grain converted rice will do.

Serves 8   Serving Size: 1/8 recipe

- 1 1/2 cups cooked rice
- 1/2 tsp salt (optional)
- Freshly ground pepper to taste
- 1/2 cup chives
- 1 oz egg substitute
- Nonfat cooking spray

1. Mix rice, salt, pepper, chives, and egg substitute.

2. Turn into a 9-inch pie shell that has been sprayed with cooking spray. Press mixture into the bottom and up sides of pie plate, using the back of a wet spoon. Do not prebake.

Exchanges
1 Starch

Calories 42
   Calories from Fat . . . 2
Total Fat . . . . 0 g
   Saturated Fat . . . . . . 0 g
Cholesterol . . . . 0 mg
Sodium . . . . 140 mg
   W/o added salt . . . . . 7 mg
Carbohydrate . . . . 9 g
   Dietary Fiber . . . . . . 0 g
   Sugars . . . . 0 g
Protein . . . . 1 g

Sweet Potato Biscuits

Serves 10   Serving Size: 1 biscuit

        1 large sweet potato, baked
        1 tsp butter
           Salt (optional) and pepper to taste
   1 1/2 cups sifted flour
        2 Tbsp baking powder
     1/2 tsp salt (optional)
        1 Tbsp sugar
     1/2 cup shortening
     1/2 cup plain yogurt
           Nonfat cooking spray

1. Preheat oven to 425°. Peel and discard potato skin. Mash hot sweet potato with butter, salt, and pepper.

2. Sift flour, baking powder, salt, and sugar together. Place in the food processor. Add shortening and blend until crumbly. Add sweet potato and yogurt. Blend.

3. Turn out onto a floured board. Knead 2–3 times. Pat into a 1 1/2-inch thick disc. Using a floured cutter, or glass, cut out 10 biscuits. Spray a baking sheet with nonfat cooking spray. Place biscuits on sheet, bake 12–15 minutes.

Exchanges
1 1/2 Starch
1 1/2 Fat

Calories 190
    Calories from Fat . . 90
Total Fat . . . . 10 g
    Saturated Fat . . . . . . 3 g
Cholesterol . . . . 1 mg
Sodium . . . . 183 mg
    W/o added salt . . . . 23 mg
Carbohydrate . . . . . . 20 g
    Dietary Fiber . . . . . . 1 g
    Sugars . . . . 3 g
Protein . . . . 3 g

Rhode Island Chicken Pie

Serves 8   Serving Size: 1/8 recipe

>   2 (3 1/2 lb) chickens, cut in pieces, skin removed
>   1 onion, chopped
>   1 tsp salt (optional)
>   Freshly ground pepper to taste
>   4 cups water
>   2 Tbsp canola oil
>   4 Tbsp flour
>   2 cups red potatoes, skins on, cubed
>   1 tsp marjoram
>   1 bay leaf
>   2 stalks celery, chopped
>   2 cups baby carrots
>   2 slices zest of lemon
>   1/2 cup chopped fresh parsley
>   Plain crust, p. 2
>   1 egg white beaten with 1 Tbsp water

1. Place all parts of the chicken except the 2 breasts in a heavy casserole. Add onion, salt, and pepper. Pour on water. Cover and simmer 30 minutes. Add chicken breasts, and cook 10 minutes.

2. Remove chicken pieces from boiling liquids and set aside. Heat oil in a saucepan. Add flour and cook, stirring, 2–3 minutes. Turn off heat. Remove 2 cups of boiling liquid, and pour over the flour-oil mixture, all at once. Beat vigorously with a wire whisk to prevent lumping. Pour this into liquid in the casserole.

3. Return chicken to the pot. Add potatoes, marjoram, bay leaf, celery, carrots, zest of lemon, and parsley. Return to heat and simmer, stirring occasionally, for 15 minutes.

4. Roll out dough to fit top of the casserole with a 2-inch overhang.
Drape over casserole, fold overhang up over edges and crimp.
Brush with egg wash. Cut a slash in the crust to allow steam to escape.
Bake in a preheated 425° oven for 15 minutes, or until top is browned.

Exchanges

1 1/2 Starch	5 Lean Meat
1 Vegetable	1/2 Fat

Calories 460
   Calories from Fat . .171
Total Fat . . . . .19 g
   Saturated Fat . . . . . . .4 g
Cholesterol . . . . .115 mg
Sodium . . . . .451 mg
   W/o added salt . . . .127 mg
Carbohydrate . . . . . . .28 g
   Dietary Fiber . . . . . . .2 g
   Sugars . . . . .2 g
Protein . . . . .41 g

Old-Fashioned Chicken Pot Pie with Cornmeal Crust

Serves 8   Serving Size: 1/8 recipe

          1 (3 1/2 lb) chicken
          4 cups water
          1 tsp salt (optional)
          1 onion, coarsely chopped
          1 carrot, coarsely chopped
          1 celery stalk, coarsely chopped
             Nonfat cooking spray
          1 onion, chopped
          2 cups diced turnip
          3 carrots, scraped and diced
          1 lb red potatoes, skins on, cubed
          2 celery stalks, diced
          3 cups chicken broth
     1/2 cup flour
          1 cup low-fat milk
          1 cup frozen peas
             Freshly ground pepper to taste
             Cornmeal crust, p. 5
          1 egg white, beaten with 1 Tbsp water

1. Place chicken in a large pot. Add water, salt, onion, carrot, and celery. Bring to boil, reduce heat to simmer, cover, and cook 45 minutes. Remove chicken and drain. Cool.

2. Strain liquid to remove vegetables and place liquid in freezer or refrigerator until fat hardens. Discard fat. Taste stock; if too mild, cook over high heat until it measures only 3 cups. Remove skin from chicken and discard. Remove meat from bones and set aside. Preheat oven to 425°.

3. Heat a large nonstick skillet sprayed with cooking spray. Add onion and cook until limp. Spray again. Add turnip, carrot, potatoes, and celery. Cook, stirring, 5 minutes. Pour stock over all. Cover and simmer 15 minutes.

4. Beat flour into milk. Add to vegetables and mix well. Cook 5 minutes. Add peas, chicken, and pepper. Turn into casserole. Roll dough out to fit top of casserole with a 2-inch overhang. Fold overhang and crimp attractively. Slash a vent to allow steam to escape. Brush with egg wash. Bake 15 minutes, or until pastry is browned.

Exchanges

1 Starch	3 Lean Meat
1 Vegetable	1 Fat

Calories 478
  Calories from Fat . .144
Total Fat . . . . .16 g
  Saturated Fat . . . . . . .4 g
Cholesterol . . . . .81 mg
Sodium . . . . .581 mg
  W/o added salt . . . .223 mg
Carbohydrate . . . . . . .48 g
  Dietary Fiber . . . . . . .6 g
  Sugars . . . . .6 g
Protein . . . . .35 g

Deep-Dish Broccoli and Leek Pie

Serves 8 Serving Size: 1/8 recipe

1 (4–5 lb) chicken, cut in pieces, skin removed
1 onion, quartered
2 cups baby carrots
1 stalk celery, cut in chunks
2 sprigs parsley
1 bay leaf
5 peppercorns
1 tsp salt (optional)
2 Tbsp olive oil
1 leek, washed, cut into 1/4-inch rings
2 cloves garlic, crushed
1/4 cup chopped fresh basil
4 Tbsp flour
2 cups broth from chicken, boiling
1 cup dry white wine
1/2 tsp salt (optional)
1/2 tsp white pepper
2 cups broccoli florets
Sweet potato biscuits, p. 7
1/2 cup chopped fresh parsley

1. Place first 8 ingredients in a large pot. Pour 8 cups water over all.
   Bring to a boil, reduce heat to simmer, cover and cook 45 minutes.
   Remove chicken, cover with plastic wrap, and set aside.

2. Strain broth. Remove carrots and set aside. Place broth in the
   refrigerator until fat hardens. Remove fat. Taste stock, and if too mild,
   reduce over high heat until it has a good strong chicken flavor. Remove
   meat from chicken bones and set aside.

3. Heat oil in a 3-quart saucepan. Add leek and sauté 4–5 minutes. Add garlic and sauté 1–2 minutes, stirring. Add basil and cook, stirring, 1 minute. Sprinkle with flour and cook, stirring, 2–3 minutes. Remove from heat and pour boiling broth in all at once. Beat vigorously with a wire whisk to prevent lumping. Return to heat and cook, stirring, until thickened.

4. Add wine, salt, and pepper. Cook broccoli in a steamer until just tender. Add to leek sauce. Add chicken and carrots. Bring to the boil, lower heat and simmer, stirring often, until heated through. Make biscuits. Place lower half of one on a serving plate and pour a serving of sauce over this. Top with other half of biscuit, sprinkle with parsley, and serve at once.

Exchanges
2 Vegetable
4 Lean Meat

Calories 324
  Calories from Fat . .108
Total Fat . . . . .12 g
  Saturated Fat . . . . . . .3 g
Cholesterol . . . . . . .103 mg
Sodium . . . . .516 mg
  W/o added salt . . . .115 mg
Carbohydrate . . . . . . .12 g
  Dietary Fiber . . . . . . .2 g
Protein . . . . .36 g

Baked Chicken Dishes

Deep-Dish Chicken Pie with Potato Crust

Serves 8   Serving Size: 1/8 recipe

2	(3 1/2 lb) chickens, cut into pieces
2	onions, chopped, divided
3	carrots, in 2-inch lengths
2	sprigs parsley
1	bay leaf
2	stalks celery, chopped, divided
1	tsp salt (optional)
1/4	tsp thyme
5	peppercorns
4	cups water
2	Tbsp canola oil
3	Tbsp flour
	Dash white pepper and nutmeg
1	cup peas
	Nonfat cooking spray
1/2	lb mushrooms, quartered
	Potato crust, p. 3
1	oz egg substitute

1. Place chicken, 1 onion, carrots, parsley, bay leaf, 1 stalk celery, salt, thyme, and peppercorns in deep pot. Add water. Bring to boil. Reduce heat, cover, and simmer 1 1/4 hours.

2. Remove chicken, strain stock. Discard all vegetables except carrots. Place stock in refrigerator until fat hardens. Skim off fat and discard. If too mild, reduce over high heat until desired strength. Put 2 cups in small pan and freeze rest for future use.

3. Remove skin from cooked chicken and discard skin. Remove flesh from bones and set aside. Mash carrots and set aside. Bring two cups of broth to a boil in a small saucepan.

4. Heat oil in 3-quart casserole. Add rest of onion and celery and cook until onion is limp. Sprinkle with flour, pepper, and nutmeg. Cook 2–3 minutes. Remove from heat, add boiling broth, beating vigorously with a whisk to prevent lumps. Return to heat and cook, stirring, until thickened. Add chicken pieces, carrots, and peas.

5. Spray nonstick skillet with cooking spray. Sauté mushrooms 5 minutes, stirring. Add to casserole.

6. Roll pastry to fit top of casserole, with 2-inch overhang. Fold overhang and crimp it. Brush pastry with egg substitute. Slash the center to allow steam to escape. Dish can be refrigerated and baked before serving. Place in a preheated 425° oven and bake 25–30 minutes or until top is golden and filling bubbly.

Exchanges

1 1/2 Starch	5 Lean Meat
1 Vegetable	

Calories 411	
Calories from Fat . . 126	
Total Fat . . . . 14 g	
Saturated Fat . . . . . . 4 g	
Cholesterol . . . . 118 mg	
Sodium . . . . 741 mg	
W/o added salt . . . 148 mg	
Carbohydrate . . . . . . 26 g	
Dietary Fiber . . . . . . 4 g	
Sugars . . . . 5 g	
Protein . . . . 44 g	

Tarte au Poulet

Serves 8   Serving Size: 1/8 recipe

1	plain crust, p. 2
	Nonfat cooking spray
4	dried porcini or shiitake mushrooms
2	shallots, thinly sliced
1	clove garlic, crushed
1/2	lb spinach
1	cup chopped cooked chicken
1	tomato, peeled, seeded, chopped
1/2	tsp rosemary
1	tsp salt (optional)
1/2	tsp white pepper
1/4	cup dry white wine
1/4	cup water from mushrooms
3/4	cup evaporated fat-free milk
12	oz egg substitute
2	Tbsp grated gruyere or Swiss cheese
1/4	tsp grated nutmeg

1. Roll pastry to fit 9-inch pie plate. Crimp edges. Press aluminum foil in bottom of pie shell, then fill with dried beans. Place in preheated 425° oven and bake 10 minutes. Cool, remove foil and beans, and set aside. Cut 3 leaf shapes from pastry scraps. Set aside.

2. Soak mushrooms in warm water to cover for 30 minutes. Drain, save liquid, and chop. Preheat oven to 325°.

3. Spray nonstick skillet with cooking spray and set on medium-high heat. Cook shallots and garlic for 1–2 minutes. Wash spinach and drain, squeezing out water. Chop finely. Spray shallot mixture with cooking spray. Add spinach and cook, covered, 2–3 minutes. Add mushrooms and cook, uncovered, 2–3 minutes, stirring.

4. Place chicken in bottom of cooked pie shell. Add spinach mixture and scatter tomato over top. Add rosemary, salt, and pepper.

5. Mix wine, mushroom water, milk, and egg substitute. Pour over all. Sprinkle cheese on top, then nutmeg. Bake for 30 minutes. Place leaf shapes on top and bake 15 minutes. Wait 10 minutes before slicing.

Exchanges

1 Starch	2 Fat
2 Meat	

Calories 246
   Calories from Fat . . 99
Total Fat . . . . 11 g
   Saturated Fat . . . . . . 3 g
Cholesterol . . . . 23 mg
Sodium . . . . 343 mg
   W/o added salt . . . . 97 mg
Carbohydrate . . . . . . 19 g
   Dietary Fiber . . . . . . 1 g
   Sugars . . . . 1 g
Protein . . . . 16 g

Vegetable Tarte au Riz

Serves 8   Serving Size: 1/8 tarte

1	1-lb eggplant, skin on, thinly sliced
1	tsp salt
1	boneless, skinless chicken breast, halved
	Butter-flavored nonfat cooking spray
1/2	lb mushrooms, sliced
1	onion, finely sliced
1	clove garlic, crushed
1	cup chopped red bell pepper
1	cup sliced zucchini
1	prebaked rice crust, p. 6
	Salt (optional) and pepper to taste
1	Tbsp chopped fresh basil
1	small tomato, peeled, chopped
1	cup evaporated fat-free milk
1	tsp liquid chicken bouillon
4	oz egg substitute
2	Tbsp grated Parmesan cheese

1. Place layer of eggplant in colander. Sprinkle with salt. Place another layer of eggplant over this. Sprinkle with salt. Repeat until all eggplant is in. Place plate over eggplant. Weight with a heavy can and let stand 30 minutes, to take out the bitter liquid. Rinse well and set aside. Preheat oven to 325°.

2. Place chicken breast halves between 2 sheets wax paper or plastic wrap. Tap with wooden mallet until chicken is 1/4-inch thick. Slice into 2 × 1-inch pieces.

3. Spray nonstick skillet with cooking spray and put over medium-high heat. Add chicken. Lower heat and cook 2–3 minutes on each side. Remove from skillet. Spray again. Sauté mushrooms 4–5 minutes. Remove. Spray skillet again and add eggplant. Cook in one layer, 5 minutes on each side. Remove cooked eggplant from pan. Repeat until all eggplant is cooked. Spray skillet again, add onions, and cook until limp. Add garlic, bell pepper, and zucchini. Cook, stirring, 5–6 minutes. Remove from heat.

4. Place mushrooms in rice shell. Cover with chicken. Sprinkle with salt, pepper, and basil. Top with onion-zucchini mixture and eggplant. Scatter tomato. Mix milk, bouillon, and egg substitute. Pour over all. Sprinkle with Parmesan cheese. Bake 45 minutes. Let sit 10 minutes before slicing.

Exchanges
1 Starch
1 Vegetable
1 Very Lean Meat

Calories 159
   Calories from Fat . . 18
Total Fat . . . . 2 g
   Saturated Fat . . . . . . 1 g
Cholesterol . . . . 21 mg
Sodium . . . . 409 mg
   W/o added salt . . . 209 mg
Carbohydrate . . . . . . 21 g
   Dietary Fiber . . . . . . 1 g
   Sugars . . . . 2 g
Protein . . . . 15 g

Chicken Turnovers

Serves 6   Serving Size: 2 turnovers

12 sheets phyllo dough
   Nonfat cooking spray
1 onion, chopped
1 clove garlic, crushed
1 tsp oregano
1 tsp salt
   Freshly ground pepper to taste
1 10 1/2-oz pkg chopped spinach, defrosted, well drained
1 lb ground chicken, p. 113
8 oz fat-free ricotta cheese
1 oz egg substitute

1. Lay phyllo sheets on a board. Cut lengthwise into two halves. Stack, wrap in plastic wrap, and cover with a damp towel. Set aside.

2. Spray nonstick skillet with cooking spray and sauté onion until limp. Add garlic, oregano, salt, pepper, and spinach. Spray again and cook, stirring, 5 minutes. Remove from pan. Spray pan again and cook chicken until browned.

3. Put chicken in bowl. Add onion mixture and mix well. Add cheese and egg. Mix well.

4. Lay one strip of phyllo on a board. Spray with cooking spray. Top with another strip of phyllo and spray. Place spoonful of filling on narrow end of strip. Fold one corner of phyllo diagonally over mixture, forming an angle (1). Fold again diagonally (2). Continue to end of strip.

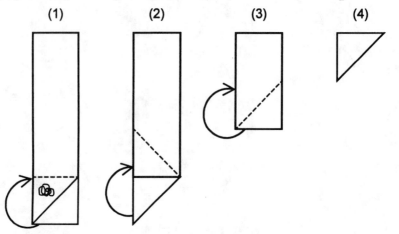

5. Spray a baking sheet. Lay turnovers side by side on sheet. Spray. Place in preheated 375° oven and bake 15–20 minutes or until brown.

Exchanges
1 1/2 Starch   2 Lean Meat
1 Vegetable

Calories 256
  Calories from Fat . . .36
Total Fat . . . . .4 g
  Saturated Fat . . . . . . .1 g
Cholesterol . . . . .50 mg
Sodium . . . . .644 mg
  W/o added salt 286
Carbohydrate . . . . . .27 g
  Dietary Fiber . . . . . . .0 g
  Sugars . . . . .1 g
Protein . . . . .27 g

Potato Quiche

Serves 8   Serving Size: 1/8 recipe

Nonfat cooking spray
1 onion, chopped
1 clove garlic, crushed
1/4 lb mushrooms, sliced
1 lb eggplant, chopped, skin on
1 prebaked potato crust, p. 3
2 cups cooked chicken
2 oz grated reduced-fat cheddar cheese
12 oz egg substitute
1 egg
2 cups evaporated fat-free milk
1 tsp salt (optional)
Freshly ground pepper to taste
1/2 tsp paprika

1. Preheat oven to 350°. Spray a nonstick skillet with cooking spray. Add onion and sauté until limp. Add garlic, mushrooms, and eggplant. Cook over medium heat, stirring constantly and spraying as needed until eggplant is soft. Put into pie shell.

2. Scatter chicken over vegetables. Top with cheese. Beat egg substitute and egg with milk, and add salt and pepper. Pour over vegetable-chicken mixture. Sprinkle with paprika. Bake 40–45 minutes, or until a knife inserted in the middle comes out clean. Let rest a good 10 minutes before slicing.

Exchanges

1 Starch	1 Vegetable
1/2 Milk	2 Lean Meat

Calories 265
　Calories from Fat . . 45
Total Fat . . . . 5 g
　Saturated Fat . . . . . . 2 g
Cholesterol . . . . 59 mg
Sodium . . . . 769 mg
　W/o added salt . . . 236 mg
Carbohydrate . . . . . . 27 g
　Dietary Fiber . . . . . . 2 g
　Sugars . . . . 2 g
Protein . . . . 28 g

Crustless Ricotta Chicken Tart with Black Olives

Serves 8   Serving Size: 1/8 tart

Nonfat cooking spray
2 cups salt-free cracker crumbs
1 1/2 tsp oregano
Freshly ground pepper to taste
1 Tbsp butter, softened
2 lb fat-free or low-fat ricotta cheese
1/2 cup sliced black olives
1/4 cup chopped fresh basil
1 egg, beaten
4 oz egg substitute
1 tsp salt (optional)
1/2 tsp white pepper
2 cups chopped cooked chicken
2 Tbsp grated Parmesan cheese

1. Preheat oven to 350°. Spray bottom and sides of a 9-inch springform pan with cooking spray. Mix crumbs, oregano, and pepper together. Mix in softened butter and blend until crumbly. Press into bottom and up sides of pan. Bake 10 minutes. Set aside.

2. Mix cheese, olives, basil, egg, egg substitute, salt, pepper, and chicken. Turn into prepared pan. Sprinkle with Parmesan cheese.

3. Bake 45 minutes, or until a knife inserted in the middle comes out clean. Remove from oven and let stand 10 minutes. Run a knife around sides of pan, then remove tart.

Exchanges

3 1/2 Starch   1 Fat
3 Lean Meat

Calories 489
 Calories from Fat . . 153
Total Fat . . . . 17 g
 Saturated Fat . . . . . . 3 g
Cholesterol . . . . 73 mg
Sodium . . . . 531 mg
 W/o added salt . . . 264 mg
Carbohydrate . . . . . . 54 g
 Dietary Fiber . . . . . . 0 g
 Sugars . . . . 0 g
Protein . . . . 33 g

Coq au Vin

Serves 6   Serving Size: 1/6 recipe

> 1 (3 1/2 lb) chicken, cut into pieces, skin removed
> Nonfat cooking spray
> 1 onion, chopped
> 1 cup diced ham
> 1 Tbsp brandy, warmed
> 1 cup red wine
> 1 cup chicken broth
> 1 bay leaf
> Bouquet garni*
> Freshly ground pepper to taste
> Nonfat cooking spray
> 1 1/2 cups frozen small white onions
> 1 1/2 cups mushrooms, quartered
> 2 Tbsp cornstarch
> 1/2 cup red wine
> 2 Tbsp chopped fresh parsley

1. Heat broiler. Spray broiler tray with cooking spray. Add chicken pieces and brown on all sides. Remove chicken. Set oven to 300°. Heat ovenproof casserole. Spray, add onions, and cook until limp. Add ham and toss well. Add chicken pieces. Ignite brandy and pour over chicken. Add wine, broth, bay leaf, bouquet garni, and pepper. Bring to boil on top of the stove, cover, and place in oven. Bake 45 minutes. When chicken is cooked, remove from liquids with a slotted spoon. Remove bay leaf and bouquet garni and discard.

2. Meanwhile, spray nonstick skillet. Add onions and cook until browned, stirring. Add mushrooms and cook 5 minutes, stirring. Set aside.

---

*Bouquet garni: a sprig each of parsley, celery top, fresh thyme, and a bay leaf tied together with string or wrapped in cheesecloth and tied. It is used as a flavoring and removed after cooking.

3. Mix cornstarch with 1/2 cup red wine to dissolve. Pour into boiling pan liquids, stirring, over low heat until liquids are thickened and clear. Add onions and mushrooms. Return chicken to casserole. Bake covered, another 15 minutes. Sprinkle with parsley and serve.

Exchanges
1 1/2 Vegetable
4 Lean Meat

Calories 353
    Calories from Fat . . . 99
Total Fat . . . . 12 g
    Saturated Fat . . . . . . 3 g
Cholesterol . . . . 106 mg
Sodium . . . . 620 mg
Carbohydrate . . . . . . 14 g
    Dietary Fiber . . . . . . 2 g
    Sugars . . . . 1 g
Protein . . . . 36 g

Chicken Wings
with Peach Dipping Sauce
(Appetizer)

Serves 12   Serving Size: 1 piece

> 3 lb chicken wings
> Nonfat cooking spray
> 1/2 tsp salt (optional) and pepper to taste
> 1 1-lb can water-pack sliced peaches, drained
> 1 small red bell pepper
> 2 cloves garlic, crushed
> 1/3 cup cider vinegar
> 1 Tbsp horseradish
> 1/3 cup brown sugar
> 1/2–1 Tbsp dry mustard
> 1/8 tsp hot pepper sauce
> 1/4 tsp salt (optional)

1. Remove wing tips (can use for soup stock). Separate wings at joints. Use little drumsticks only. Remove skin. Spray shallow pan and place "drumsticks" side by side. Spray. Season with salt and pepper. Broil 5 inches from flame 5–7 minutes on each side. Transfer to shallow baking dish. Set oven to 375°.

2. Place peaches, red bell pepper, garlic, vinegar, horseradish, brown sugar, mustard, and hot pepper sauce in the jar of a blender or food processor. Puree until smooth. Pour into a saucepan, bring to boil, stirring. Reduce heat to simmer and cook 5 minutes, or until slightly thickened. Reserve 1 cup of sauce for dipping and pour rest over chicken wings, coating well. Bake 35–40 minutes, turning several times.

Exchanges
2 Lean Meat

Calories 159
  Calories from Fat . . 45
Total Fat . . . . 5 g
  Saturated Fat . . . . . . 1 g
Cholesterol . . . . 49 mg
Sodium . . . . 202 mg
  W/o added salt . . . . 69 mg
Carbohydrate . . . . 9 g
  Dietary Fiber . . . . . . 0 g
  Sugars . . . . 2 g
Protein . . . . 18 g

Basic Crepe Recipe

Crepe batter must stand at least 2 hours before using. This allows the flour to absorb the liquids, so you can make these paper-thin pancakes.

Serves 16   Serving Size: 1 crepe

> 1 cup water
> 1 cup fat-free milk
> 8 oz egg substitute
> 1/2 tsp salt (optional)
> 2 cups flour
> 1 Tbsp butter, melted
>   Nonfat cooking spray

1. Place water, milk, egg substitute, and salt in a blender or food processor. Blend. Add flour gradually, scraping down sides occasionally. Add butter. Let stand at least 2 hours before continuing.

2. Use a 6-inch nonstick frying pan and an 8-inch nonstick frying pan. Heat smaller pan over medium heat. Spray with cooking spray. Pour a large spoonful of batter into pan and swirl around to cover the surface. Cook until completely set. Loosen edges of crepe with a spatula. Turn upside down over larger pan that has been heated and sprayed with cooking spray.

When crepe falls into larger pan, allow to cook on other side 2–3 minutes. The first couple of crepes may not turn out well. Once the pans temper, the crepes will be good. Repeat steps until all batter is used. Stack crepes together and wrap in plastic wrap until ready to use.

Exchanges

1 Starch

Calories 75
   Calories from Fat 9
Total Fat . . . . .1 g
   Saturated Fat . . . . . . .0 g
Cholesterol . . . . .2 mg
Sodium . . . . .103 mg
   W/o added salt . . . . .36 mg
Carbohydrate . . . . . . .13 g
   Dietary Fiber . . . . . . .0 g
   Sugars . . . . .0 g
Protein . . . . .3 g

Swedish Pancakes

Serves 8   Serving Size: 2 crepes

Nonfat cooking spray
1 onion, chopped
1/4 lb mushrooms, chopped
1 clove garlic, crushed
1/2 tsp salt (optional)
Freshly ground pepper to taste
2 cups chopped cooked chicken
1/4 cup chopped fresh parsley
2 Tbsp grated Parmesan cheese
1 1/2 cup thick béchamel sauce, p. 30
16 crepes, p. 27
Nonfat cooking spray
1 egg yolk
1/2 cup evaporated fat-free milk
1/4 cup sherry
2 Tbsp grated Parmesan cheese

1. Spray a nonstick skillet. Over medium heat, sauté onion until limp. Add mushrooms and cook 5 minutes. Add garlic and sauté 1 minute. Add salt, pepper, chicken, parsley, and cheese. Add 1/4 cup béchamel sauce. Fill each crepe with a spoonful of this filling. Preheat oven to 350°.

2. Spray shallow baking dish. Roll crepes and place, seam side down in this dish. Beat egg yolk, milk, and sherry into remaining béchamel sauce. Pour over crepes, and sprinkle with cheese. Bake 15 minutes or until hot and bubbly. Run quickly under the broiler if not browned.

Exchanges
2 Starch
3 Lean Meat

Calories 347
  Calories from Fat . . 90
Total Fat . . . . 10 g
  Saturated Fat . . . . . . 3 g
Cholesterol . . . . 71 mg
Sodium . . . . 600 mg
  W/o added salt . . . 200 mg
Carbohydrate . . . . . . 34 g
  Dietary Fiber . . . . . . 2 g
  Sugars . . . . 4 g
Protein . . . . 25 g

Crepes with Chicken, Mushroom, and Eggplant

Serves 8   Serving Size: 1/8 recipe

Filling #1

Nonfat cooking spray
1 cup finely chopped onion
1 cup finely chopped celery
1/2 cup finely chopped red bell pepper
1/2 cup finely chopped ham
2 cups finely chopped cooked chicken
1/2 cup thick béchamel sauce (recipe follows)

1. Heat a nonstick skillet. Spray with cooking spray. Over medium-high heat, cook onion, celery, red bell pepper, and ham, stirring, 5 minutes. Mix in chicken and béchamel sauce.

Filling #2

Nonfat cooking spray
3 shallots, chopped
1 lb mushrooms, finely chopped
2 cloves garlic, crushed
1 cup peeled, finely chopped eggplant
1/2 tsp salt (optional)
Freshly ground pepper
1/2 cup thick béchamel sauce (recipe follows)

1. Heat a nonstick skillet. Spray with cooking spray. Add shallots, mushrooms, garlic, and eggplant. Cook over medium heat, stirring, until eggplant is soft, spraying again as needed. Stir in salt, pepper, and béchamel sauce.

Sauce for Crepes

1 1/2 cups thick béchamel sauce (recipe below)
3/4 cup evaporated fat-free milk
1/4 cup dry sherry

1. Wisk all 3 ingredients together until smooth.

Thick Béchamel Sauce

6 Tbsp canola oil
6 Tbsp flour
2 cups fat-free milk, scalded
1 tsp salt (optional)
1/4 tsp white pepper
1/2 tsp ground nutmeg

1. Heat oil in a saucepan. Add flour and cook, stirring, 2–3 minutes. Remove from heat and pour on scalded milk all at once. Beat vigorously with wire whisk to prevent lumping. Add seasonings. Return to heat and cook until very thick. Makes 2 1/2 cups.

To Assemble Crepes

Nonfat cooking spray

9 salt-free crepes, p. 27

All the above recipes

3 Tbsp grated Parmesan cheese

3 Tbsp chopped fresh parsley

1. Preheat oven to 350°. Spray the bottom of an ovenproof 12-inch dish with cooking spray. Place 1 crepe in the bottom. Spread with filling #1. Lay a crepe on top. Spread with filling #2. Top with another crepe and spread with filling #1. Repeat, alternating fillings until all crepes are used, ending with a crepe on top.

2. Pour sauce over the crepes. Sprinkle with Parmesan cheese and bake 25 minutes. Sprinkle with parsley and serve, cut in wedges.

Exchanges

1 1/2 Starch	2 Lean Meat
1/2 Skim Milk	1 1/2 Fat
1 Vegetable	

Calories 367
  Calories from Fat . . 130
Total Fat . . . . 14 g
  Saturated Fat . . . . . . 2 g
Cholesterol . . . . 45 mg
Sodium . . . . 679 mg
  W/o added salt . . . 280 mg
Carbohydrate . . . . . . 31 g
  Dietary Fiber . . . . . . 2 g
  Sugars . . . . 6 g
Protein . . . . 26 g

Sesame-Baked Chicken Breasts with Chutney

This is a quick and easy recipe. Great for those busy days.

Serves 4   Serving Size: 1/4 recipe

- 1/2 cup flour
- 1 tsp salt (optional)
- 1/4 tsp pepper
- 1 tsp garlic powder
- 1/2 tsp oregano
- 2 boneless, skinless chicken breasts, halved
- 1/4 cup egg substitute
- 1 cup sesame seeds
- Nonfat cooking spray
- 1 jar commercial chutney

1. Preheat the oven to 350°. Mix flour, salt, pepper, garlic powder, and oregano. Roll chicken breasts in this mixture. Shake off excess. Mix egg substitute with 2 tablespoons water. Dip chicken breasts in this mixture, then roll in sesame seeds.

2. Spray a 9 × 9-inch baking pan with cooking spray. Lay chicken breasts, side by side, in this pan. Spray with cooking spray. Bake 25 minutes. Place a spoonful of chutney under each chicken breast and serve.

Exchanges

1 Starch   4 Very Lean Meat
1 1/2 Fruit 1 Fat

Calories 366
  Calories from Fat . . 90
Total Fat . . . . 10 g
  Saturated Fat . . . . . . 2 g
Cholesterol . . . . 73 mg
Sodium . . . . 628 mg
  W/o added salt . . . . 94 mg
Carbohydrate . . . . . . 35 g
  Dietary Fiber . . . . . . 3 g
  Sugars . . . . 19 g
Protein . . . . 32 g

*B*raised Chicken Dishes

In braising, the chicken is simmered in a bath of liquid, along with condiments, aromatic herbs, and vegetables. The liquid can be stock, broth, wine, or water.

Braised Chinese Chicken

Serves 8   Serving Size: 1/8 recipe

> 1 (4–5 lb) chicken, cut into pieces, skin removed
> 4 green onions, cut into 2-inch pieces
> 2 Tbsp fresh ginger, grated
> 1 garlic clove, crushed
> 1 cup low-sodium chicken stock
> 1/2 cup lite soy sauce
> 1/4 tsp freshly ground pepper
> 1/4 cup sherry
> 1 tsp sugar

1. Place chicken under a heated broiler and brown on both sides, about 10 minutes. Place green onions, ginger, garlic, chicken stock, soy sauce, and pepper in large pot. Bring to boil, reduce heat to simmer, and cook 4–5 minutes.

2. Add browned chicken. Cover and simmer 25 minutes. Turn occasionally. Add sherry and sugar. Simmer another 25 minutes, tightly covered. Add a little water if liquids dry out during cooking.

Exchanges
3 Lean Meat

Calories 200
   Calories from Fat . . 62
Total Fat . . . . 7 g
   Saturated Fat . . . . . . 2 g
Cholesterol . . . . 81 mg
Sodium . . . . 687 mg
Carbohydrate . . . . 4 g
   Dietary Fiber . . . . . . 0 g
   Sugars . . . . 1 g
Protein . . . . 28 g

Brunswick Stew

Serves 6   Serving Size: 1/6 recipe

- 1 Tbsp canola oil
- 2 onions, sliced
- 1 green bell pepper, chopped
- 1 clove garlic, crushed
- Nonfat cooking spray
- 1 (4 lb) chicken, cut into pieces, skin removed
- 1 tsp salt (optional)
- Freshly ground pepper
- 3 cups low-fat, low-sodium chicken broth
- 3 tomatoes, peeled, seeded, chopped
- 1 cup white wine
- 1 Tbsp Worcestershire sauce
- 1 lb fresh lima beans, or 1 10 1/2-oz pkg frozen
- 1/2 cup sliced okra, fresh or frozen
- 1 cup corn niblets, frozen or canned
- 1/4 cup chopped fresh parsley

1. Heat oil in nonstick skillet. Add onions and bell pepper. Sauté over medium heat until onion is limp. Add garlic and sauté 1 minute.

2. Spray a heated broiler tray and broil chicken until browned on all sides. Place in a large heavy-bottomed kettle.

3. Add onion mixture, salt, pepper, broth, tomatoes, wine, and Worcestershire sauce. Bring to boil, reduce to simmer, and cook, covered, 30 minutes. Add lima beans, okra, and corn. Bring to boil and simmer another 20 minutes. Stir in parsley, and serve.

Exchanges

3 Starch	4 Lean Meat
1 Vegetable	

Calories 520
   Calories from Fat . .108
Total Fat . . . . .12 g
   Saturated Fat . . . . . . .3 g
Cholesterol . . . . .92 mg
Sodium . . . . .545 mg
   W/o added salt . . . .190 mg
Carbohydrate . . . . . . .61 g
   Dietary Fiber . . . . . .17 g
   Sugars . . . . .7 g
Protein . . . . .45 g

Chicken Fricassee with Dumplings

Serves 8   Serving Size: 1/8 recipe

1/4 cup flour
1 tsp marjoram
1/4 tsp ground thyme
1 (4 lb) chicken, cut into pieces, skin removed
Nonfat cooking spray
6–8 cups boiling water
1 tsp salt (optional)
Freshly ground pepper
1 cup baby carrots
2 cups pearl onions, peeled
1 stalk celery, chopped
1/2 lb mushrooms, quartered
1/4 cup chopped parsley
Dumplings (next recipe)

1. Place flour, marjoram, and thyme in a zippered plastic bag. Shake. Add chicken pieces, and shake again to coat. Heat a large deep kettle with a lid. Spray, add chicken, and brown on all sides over medium heat. Spray again, if necessary.

2. Pour 6–8 cups boiling water over chicken, almost to cover it. Add salt, pepper, carrots, onions, and celery. Bring to boil, lower heat, and simmer 1 hour.

3. Meanwhile, spray nonstick skillet. Add mushrooms and cook, stirring, 5 minutes. Set aside. Add mushrooms and parsley to cooked chicken. Drop dumpling batter by teaspoonful on top. Cover and simmer 20 minutes without removing the lid.

Exchanges
1 Vegetable
4 Lean Meat

Calories 235
   Calories from Fat . . 72
Total Fat . . . . 8 g
   Saturated Fat . . . . . . 2 g
Cholesterol . . . . 92 mg
Sodium . . . . 358 mg
   W/o added salt . . . . 92 mg
Carbohydrate . . . . 8 g
   Dietary Fiber . . . . . . 2 g
   Sugars . . . . 3 g
Protein . . . . 32 g

Dumplings

Serves 8   Serving Size: 1 dumpling

    1 cup sifted flour

1/2 tsp salt (optional)

    2 tsp baking powder

1/2 Tbsp shortening

    1 egg, beaten

    6 Tbsp fat-free milk

1. Sift flour, salt, and baking powder together. Place in food processor. Add shortening and blend until crumbly. Beat egg and milk together and add. Drop 8 large teaspoons of batter on top of fricasee.

Exchanges

1 Starch

Calories	75
Calories from Fat	9
Total Fat	1 g
Saturated Fat	0 g
Cholesterol	15 mg
Sodium	148 mg
W/o added salt	15 mg
Carbohydrate	13 g
Dietary Fiber	0 g
Sugars	1 g
Protein	2 g

Medallion Sauce

Serving Size: 3 Tbsp

Nonfat cooking spray
1 onion, finely chopped
1 clove garlic, crushed
2 cups chicken liquids from medallions, boiling
2 Tbsp quick-mixing flour
1/2 cup fat-free or reduced-fat sour cream
Salt (optional) and pepper to taste
2 Tbsp chopped fresh parsley

1. Spray a saucepan with cooking spray. Add onion and sauté over medium heat until limp. Add garlic and cook 1–2 minutes, stirring. Pour on boiling liquid. Simmer 5 minutes.

2. Beat flour into sour cream in a bowl. Remove pan from heat and beat sour cream mixture vigorously into liquids with a wire whisk. Return to heat and cook, stirring, until thickened. Stir in salt, pepper, and parsley. Makes 2 1/2 cups.

Exchanges
Free

Calories 20
 Calories from Fat . . . 3
Total Fat . . . . 0 g
 Saturated Fat . . . . . . 0 g
Cholesterol . . . . 0 mg
Sodium . . . . 75 mg
 W/o added salt . . . . 22 mg
Carbohydrate . . . . 4 g
 Dietary Fiber . . . . . . 0 g
 Sugars . . . . 0 g
Protein . . . . 2 g

Chicken Maryland

Serves 8   Serving Size: 1/8 recipe

- 3/4 cup flour
- 1 tsp salt (optional)
- Freshly ground pepper
- 1 tsp paprika
- 2 (3 lb) chickens, cut in pieces, skin removed
- Nonfat cooking spray
- 2 cups low-sodium chicken broth
- 4 cups vegetables of choice

1. Place flour, salt, pepper, and paprika in a zippered plastic bag. Add chicken pieces and shake to coat. Spray a large nonstick skillet with cooking spray. Add chicken pieces and brown over medium heat on all sides.

2. Add broth, bring to the boil, reduce heat to simmer, cover, and cook 30 minutes. Add vegetables, cover, and cook until vegetables are tender.

Exchanges
1 Vegetable
4 Lean Meat

Calories 292
   Calories from Fat . . 90
Total Fat . . . . 10 g
   Saturated Fat . . . . . 2.5 g
Cholesterol . . . . 115 mg
Sodium 392
   W/o added salt . . . 125 mg
Carbohydrate . . . . 9 g
   Dietary Fiber . . . . . . 2 g
   Sugars . . . . 1 g
Protein . . . . 40 g

Chicken L'Espagnol

Serves 8   Serving Size: 1/8 recipe

1/4	cup flour
1	tsp salt (optional)
	Freshly ground pepper
1	(5 lb) chicken, cut in pieces, skin removed
	Nonfat cooking spray
2	onions, sliced
1	green bell pepper, diced
1	red bell pepper, diced
1	clove garlic, crushed
2	cups tomatoes, peeled, seeded, chopped
2	cups low-sodium chicken broth
1	tsp sugar
1	tsp salt (optional)
1/2	tsp pepper
1 1/2	cups mushrooms, sliced
2	cups frozen peas
1/2	cup sliced green olives (optional)

1. Mix flour, salt, and pepper. Roll chicken pieces in this mixture. Spray large heavy-bottomed pot with cooking spray and using medium heat, brown chicken pieces on all sides. Remove from pot.

2. Spray again. Add onions and bell peppers and sauté until onions are limp. Add garlic, tomatoes, broth, sugar, salt, and pepper. Return chicken to pot. Bring to boil. Reduce heat to simmer and cook 40 minutes.

3. Meanwhile, spray a nonstick skillet and sauté mushrooms, 5 minutes. Set aside. Add mushrooms, peas, and olives to chicken after 40 minutes. Cook another 7–8 minutes.

Exchanges

1/2 Starch	3 Lean Meat
1 Vegetable	

Calories 274
   Calories from Fat . . 77
Total Fat . . . . 9 g
   Saturated Fat . . . . . . 2 g
Cholesterol . . . . 81 mg
Sodium . . . . 880 mg
   W/o added salt
   and olives . . . . 347 mg
Carbohydrate . . . . . . 17 g
   Dietary Fiber . . . . . . 3 g
   Sugars . . . . 6 g
Protein . . . . 31 g

Chicken Medallions with Winter Squash

Serves 6   Serving Size: 1/6 recipe

                1 1/2   lb ground chicken, p. 113
                1 1/2   cups soft bread crumbs
                    8   oz egg substitute
                    1   tsp salt (optional)
                        Freshly ground pepper
                  1/2   tsp nutmeg
                        Nonfat cooking spray
                    2   cups low-fat chicken broth
                        Paprika
                    1   butternut squash
                    2   Tbsp maple syrup
                        Salt and pepper
                    1   tsp ground ginger
                        Sauce (next recipe)

1. Preheat oven to 350°. Mix chicken, bread crumbs, egg substitute, salt, pepper, and nutmeg. Form into 12 medallions about 1/4 inch thick. Spray shallow baking dish with cooking spray. Place medallions in dish. Pour in chicken broth. Cover with aluminum foil. Bring to the boil on top of the stove, then put in oven. Braise 15 minutes.

2. Remove chicken from broth and drain on paper towels. Sprinkle with paprika. Strain liquids into a 2-cup measure, adding water to reach this mark if necessary. Set aside.

3. Cut squash into 12 1/4-inch rings. Remove rind. Spray shallow baking dish. Lay squash rings in bottom. Brush with maple syrup. Sprinkle with salt, pepper, and ginger. Spray with cooking spray. Place in oven and bake 20–25 minutes or until tender when pierced with a fork. Place a chicken medallion on each squash ring. Bake 10 minutes or until chicken is heated through. Serve with sauce on p. 38.

Exchanges
1 Starch
3 Lean Meat

Calories 248
   Calories from Fat . . 36
Total Fat . . . . 4 g
   Saturated Fat . . . . . . 1 g
Cholesterol . . . . 68 mg
Sodium . . . . 726 mg
   W/o added salt . . . 190 mg
Carbohydrate . . . . . . 20 g
   Dietary Fiber . . . . . . 2 g
   Sugars . . . . 7 g
Protein . . . . 31 g

Chicken Stew with Rice Dumplings

This is a wonderful way to use leftover rice. This dumpling recipe can also be used to make a delicious rice biscuit, light, fluffy, and satisfying.

Serves 4 Serving Size: 1/4 recipe

1	(4 lb) chicken, cut in pieces, skin removed
2 1/2	cups low-fat chicken stock
1 1/2	cups water
2	bay leaves
2	carrots
2	parsnips
2	stalks celery
1	10-oz pkg frozen pearl onions, thawed
1/2	tsp each thyme and sage
1/2	tsp salt (optional)
	Freshly ground pepper
1	10-oz pkg frozen peas
	Dumplings (next recipe)

1. Place chicken in deep kettle. Add stock and 1 1/2 cups water. Add bay leaves. Bring to the boil, reduce heat, cover, and simmer 30 minutes.

2. Peel carrots and parsnips. Cut into diagonal 1-inch pieces. Cut celery stalks into 1-inch pieces. Add to chicken. Add onions, thyme, sage, salt, and pepper. Simmer 15 minutes. Discard bay leaves, stir in peas. Add dumplings.

Exchanges

1 Starch
4 Lean Meat

Calories	289
Calories from Fat	72
Total Fat	8 g
Saturated Fat	2 g
Cholesterol	92 mg
Sodium	284 mg
W/o added salt	150 mg
Carbohydrate	19 g
Dietary Fiber	5 g
Sugars	4 g
Protein	34 g

Rice Dumplings

Serves 4   Serving Size: 1 dumpling or 1 biscuit

  1 1/3 cups cake flour, sifted
      1 cup cooked rice
      4 tsp baking powder
    1/2 tsp salt (optional)
      2 Tbsp shortening
    1/3 cup fat-free milk

1. Mix flour, rice, baking powder, and salt. Add shortening, and blend until crumbly. Add milk and blend to make sticky dough. Drop 8 teaspoons of dough on top of stew. Cover tightly and cook over low heat 15 minutes. Do not lift lid. Serve stew with 2 dumplings each.

2. To make biscuits: Flour hands. Scoop a handful of dough and form a 1 × 2-inch disc. Place on sprayed baking sheet. Repeat until all dough is used. Bake in a preheated 400° oven for 12–15 minutes. Makes 8 biscuits.

Exchanges
1 Starch
1/2 Fat

Calories 125
    Calories from Fat . . 27
Total Fat . . . . 3 g
    Saturated Fat . . . . . . 1 g
Cholesterol . . . . 0 mg
Sodium . . . . 147 mg
    W/o added salt . . . . 13 mg
Carbohydrate . . . . . . 21 g
    Dietary Fiber . . . . . . 0 g
    Sugars . . . . 0 g
Protein . . . . 2 g

Chicken Morengo

Serves 6   Serving Size: 1/6 recipe

	Nonfat cooking spray
1 1/2	lb boneless, skinless chicken breast, cubed
1	onion, finely chopped
1	clove garlic, crushed
1	carrot, chopped
1	stalk celery, chopped
1	tsp basil
1	large tomato, peeled, seeded, chopped
1/2	cup dry white wine
2	cups low-sodium chicken stock
1/2	tsp salt (optional)
	Freshly ground pepper
	Bouquet garni*
2	Tbsp cornstarch
1/2	cup white wine
	Nonfat cooking spray
1	cup frozen small white onions, thawed
1/2	lb small white mushrooms, trimmed
1/2	cup sliced black olives
2	Tbsp chopped fresh parsley

1. Preheat oven to 350°. Heat a large ovenproof casserole with a lid. Spray with cooking spray. Add chicken and brown for 5–6 minutes. Remove chicken. Spray casserole again. Add onion and cook, stirring, until limp. Add garlic, carrot, and celery. Cook 5 minutes. Add basil, and cook 1 minute. Add tomato, and cook 10 minutes, stirring.

2. Return chicken to pot. Add wine, stock, salt, pepper, and bouquet garni. Bring to boil on top of stove, cover, put in oven, and braise 30 minutes. Discard bouquet garni.

---

*Bouquet garni: a sprig each of parsley, celery top, fresh thyme, and a bay leaf tied together with string or wrapped in cheesecloth and tied. It is used as a flavoring and removed after cooking.

3. Mix cornstarch with wine until dissolved. Stir into boiling liquids in casserole. Cook on top of the stove until clear and thickened. Heat a nonstick skillet. Spray. Add onions, and cook until browned. Spray again and add mushrooms. Cook 5 minutes. Stir into chicken along with olives and parsley. Serve at once.

Exchanges
2 Vegetable   1 Fat
4 Very Lean Meat

Calories 277
   Calories from Fat . . 72
Total Fat . . . . 8 g
   Saturated Fat . . . . . . 1 g
Cholesterol . . . . 87 mg
Sodium . . . . 393 mg
   W/o added salt . . . 227 mg
Carbohydrate . . . . . . 10 g
   Dietary Fiber . . . . . . 2 g
   Sugars . . . . 2 g
Protein . . . . 36 g

Red Cooked Chinese Chicken

Serves 6   Serving Size: 1/6 recipe

- 2 Tbsp grated fresh ginger
- 2 Tbsp lite soy sauce
- 1 Tbsp sherry
- Freshly ground pepper
- 1 (3–4 lb) chicken, skin removed
- 2 Tbsp canola oil
- 1 green onion, chopped
- 2 Tbsp fresh ginger, grated
- 1/4 cup lite soy sauce
- 1 cup boiling water
- 1 tsp sugar

1. Combine ginger, soy sauce, sherry, and pepper. Rub into chicken. Place in bowl and marinate 1 hour. Heat oil in saucepan. Add green onions and ginger and sauté 1–2 minutes. Add soy sauce and cook 1–2 minutes. Hold chicken over a bowl and pour heated soy sauce into the cavity, swirling, then allowing to drain. Repeat 4–5 times, heating soy sauce mixture as needed.

2. Pour sauce into a large pot. Bring to the boil. Add chicken and cook, turning often, to brown. Add boiling water, cover, and simmer 25–30 minutes. Sprinkle with sugar, cover, and simmer another 5 minutes.

Exchanges
4 Lean Meat

Calories 234
  Calories from Fat . . 90
Total Fat . . . . 10 g
  Saturated Fat . . . . . . 2 g
Cholesterol . . . . 92 mg
Sodium . . . . 678 mg
Carbohydrate . . . . 3 g
  Dietary Fiber . . . . . . 1 g
  Sugars . . . . 1 g
Protein . . . . 31 g

New England Boiled Dinner

Serves 8 Serving Size: 1/8 recipe

1 (4 1/2 lb) chicken, skin removed
Water
1 tsp salt (optional)
24 pearl onions, peeled
Nonfat cooking spray
1 lb potatoes, peeled, quartered
12 baby carrots
1 pt brussel sprouts, cleaned, trimmed
2 cups cauliflower florets
2 Tbsp chopped fresh parsley

1. Place chicken in a 6-quart stockpot. Cover with water. Add salt. Bring to the boil, cover, and simmer 1 hour. Remove chicken from stock. Refrigerate stock. When fat has hardened, remove and discard it.

2. Cut a cross in the root end of each pearl onion. Spray a nonstick skillet with cooking spray. Add onions and cook over medium heat, until lightly browned.

3. One hour before serving, taste stock. If too mild, reduce over high heat until 4 1/2 cups remain. Remove 1 1/2 cups and reserve for horseradish sauce. Add onions, potatoes, and carrots to remaining stock. Cook 10 minutes.

4. Return chicken to pot. Add remaining vegetables, except parsley. Bring to the boil, reduce heat and simmer 15 minutes. Remove chicken and drain well. Remove vegetables with slotted spoon and place on heated platter. Place chicken on top. Sprinkle with parsley and serve with horseradish sauce.

Exchanges

1 Starch	2 Vegetable
3 Lean Meat	

Calories 281	
Calories from Fat . . .63	
Total Fat . . . . .7 g	
Saturated Fat . . . . . . .2 g	
Cholesterol . . . . .81 mg	
Sodium . . . . .380 mg	
W/o added salt . . . .113 mg	
Carbohydrate . . . . . . .23 g	
Dietary Fiber . . . . . . .5 g	
Sugars . . . . .4 g	
Protein . . . . .30 g	

Horseradish Sauce

Serving Size: 1/8 recipe

Nonfat cooking spray

2 Tbsp chopped green onions

1 clove garlic, crushed

1 1/2 cups boiling chicken stock

1 tsp sugar

1/4 tsp white pepper

2 Tbsp quick-mixing flour

3 Tbsp fat-free or reduced-fat sour cream

2 Tbsp commercial horseradish

1 Tbsp chopped capers

1. Spray a small saucepan with cooking spray. Cook green onions and garlic over medium heat, stirring, 2–3 minutes. Add boiling stock, sugar, and pepper. Mix flour with sour cream. Beat well. Stir into liquids and beat well. Cook, stirring until thickened. Stir in horseradish and capers.

Exchanges

Free

Calories 20
    Calories from Fat 2
Total Fat . . . . .0 g
    Saturated Fat . . . . . . .0 g
Cholesterol . . . . .0 mg
Sodium . . . . .96 mg
Carbohydrate . . . . . . .3 g
    Dietary Fiber . . . . . . .0 g
    Sugars . . . . .1 g
Protein . . . . .1 g

Chicken Casseroles

This chapter covers baked chicken dishes that include various condiments and aromatic herbs. They are cooked in an attractive dish that can be taken from the oven to the table and served directly to family or guests.

Chicken with Oysters

Serves 8   Serving Size: 1/8 recipe

Nonfat cooking spray
1 (3 1/2 lb) chicken, cut into pieces, skin removed
1 Tbsp oil
2 Tbsp flour
1 cup low-sodium chicken broth, boiling
1 cup evaporated fat-free milk, scalded
1/2 tsp salt (optional)
1/4 tsp white pepper
1 pt shucked oysters

1. Preheat oven to 350°. Heat broiler. Spray broiler tray. Place chicken on tray and broil until browned on all sides (5–6 minutes). Place in casserole with lid.

2. Heat oil in saucepan over medium heat. Add flour and cook, stirring, 2–3 minutes. Remove from heat and pour on boiling broth, beating vigorously to prevent lumping. Return to heat and cook until thickened. Add scalded evaporated milk, salt, and pepper. Beat until smooth. Pour over chicken.

3. Cover and bake for 35 minutes. Add oysters, cover, and bake another 10 minutes. Serve at once.

Exchanges
3 Lean Meat

Calories 228
    Calories from Fat . 79
Total Fat . . . . 9 g
    Saturated Fat . . . . . . 2 g
Cholesterol . . . . 97 mg
Sodium . . . . 370 mg
    W/o added salt . . . 237 mg
Carbohydrate . . . . 8 g
    Dietary Fiber . . . . . . 0 g
    Sugars . . . . 0 g
Protein . . . . 28 g

Chicken Jambalaya

Serves 6 Serving Size: 1/6 recipe

1	Tbsp canola oil
1	onion, finely chopped
1	clove garlic, crushed
1/2	green bell pepper, chopped
1 1/2	lb boneless, skinless chicken breasts, cubed
1 1/2	cups brown rice
3	cups low-sodium chicken broth
3	Tbsp tomato paste
1	tsp chili powder
1	tsp Worcestershire sauce
	Freshly ground pepper to taste
1/8	tsp hot pepper sauce (optional)

1. Preheat oven to 350°. Heat oil in ovenproof casserole. Add onion, garlic, and green pepper. Cook until onion is limp. Add chicken. Cook, stirring, 2–3 minutes. Add rice, and cook, stirring, 2–3 minutes.

2. Add broth, tomato paste, chili powder, Worcestershire sauce, pepper, and hot pepper sauce. Bring to the boil on top of stove, cover, and bake in oven for 45 minutes or until rice is cooked and liquid has been absorbed.

Exchanges

2 Starch	1 Vegetable
4 Lean Meat	1/2 Fat

Calories	.396
Calories from Fat . . .	.69
Total Fat	.8 g
Saturated Fat	.1 g
Cholesterol	.87 mg
Sodium	.125 mg
Carbohydrate	.41 g
Dietary Fiber	.4 g
Sugars	.1 g
Protein	.38 g

Chicken au Gratin

Serves 8   Serving Size: 1/8 recipe

  1 (4–5 lb) chicken, cut in pieces, skin removed
  1 tsp salt (optional)
1/2 tsp pepper
  1   Tbsp lemon juice
1/4 cup olive oil
     Boiling water
  1 tsp salt (optional)
  2 cups stock, from poached chicken, boiling
  2 Tbsp olive oil
  4 Tbsp flour
  1 tsp Worcestershire sauce
1/4 cup dry sherry
  2 Tbsp grated Parmesan cheese
  1 cup soft bread crumbs
  1 tsp paprika

1. Place chicken in bowl. Mix salt, pepper, lemon juice, and 1/4 cup olive oil in a jar. Shake well and pour over chicken. Cover and marinate overnight, turning once or twice. Drain well, dry with paper towels. Place chicken in large pot. Cover with boiling water, add 1 tsp salt (optional) and simmer, covered, 30 minutes. Drain well, reserving stock.

2. Skim off fat. Pour liquid into saucepan and, over high heat, reduce to 2 cups. Preheat oven to 350°. Heat 2 Tbsp olive oil in saucepan. Add flour and cook, stirring, 2–3 minutes. Remove from heat and pour in boiling stock, beating vigorously with a whisk to prevent lumping. Return to heat and cook, stirring, until thickened. Add Worcestershire sauce and sherry.

3. Place chicken in a casserole. Pour sauce over all. Bake 20 minutes. Sprinkle with cheese, bread crumbs, and paprika. Return to oven and bake, uncovered, for 15 minutes. If top is not brown enough, run under the broiler quickly.

Exchanges
1 Vegetable
4 Lean Meat
1/2 Fat

Calories	292
Calories from Fat	18
Total Fat	12 g
Saturated Fat	3 g
Cholesterol	105 mg
Sodium	416 mg
W/o added salt	150 mg
Carbohydrate	6 g
Dietary Fiber	0 g
Sugars	1 g
Protein	35 g

Hunter's Chicken

Serves 8   Serving Size: 1/8 recipe

　　　　Nonfat cooking spray
　2　(3 lb) chickens, cut in pieces, skin removed
　　　　Salt (optional) and pepper to taste
1/2　lb mushrooms, sliced
　1　large onion, sliced
　1　clove garlic, crushed
　1　tsp tarragon
1/4　tsp pepper
　1　cup white wine
　2　cups low-sodium beef broth
　1　Tbsp tomato sauce
　2　Tbsp cornstarch
1/4　cup white wine
　1　Tbsp chopped fresh parsley

1. Heat a broiler. Spray tray. Brown chicken on all sides (5–6 minutes). Place in casserole with lid. Salt and pepper to taste.

2. Preheat oven to 350°. Heat a nonstick skillet and spray well. Add mushrooms and sauté, stirring, 5 minutes. Scatter over chicken. Spray skillet again. Add onion and cook until limp. Add garlic and tarragon. Cook 1 minute. Scatter over chicken. Sprinkle with pepper. Pour wine and broth over chicken and vegetables.

3. Bring to the boil on top of the stove. Cover, place in oven, and cook 50 minutes. Stir in tomato sauce. Mix cornstarch with wine. Stir into casserole liquids. Cook on top of the stove until thickened and clear. Sprinkle with parsley.

Exchanges
1 Vegetable
5 Lean Meat

Calories 299
　Calories from Fat . . 90
Total Fat . . . . 10 g
　Saturated Fat . . . . . . 3 g
Cholesterol . . . . 115 mg
Sodium . . . . 438 mg
　W/o added salt . . . 297 mg
Carbohydrate . . . . 6 g
　Dietary Fiber . . . . . . 1 g
　Sugars . . . . 1 g
Protein . . . . 39 g

Orange Baked Chicken

This baked casserole takes about 15 minutes to prepare and 30 minutes to bake.

Serves 8   Serving Size: 1/8 recipe

> 4 boneless, skinless chicken breasts, halved
> 2 Tbsp butter, melted
> 1/2 tsp salt (optional)
>   Freshly ground pepper
> 3 Tbsp flour
> 1/2 tsp salt (optional)
> 1/4 tsp dry mustard
> 1/2 tsp cinnamon
> 1/8 tsp ground ginger
> 1 1/2 cups orange juice, boiling

1. Preheat oven to 375°. Place chicken breasts in baking dish. Brush with melted butter. Sprinkle with salt and pepper. Bake 15 minutes, uncovered.

2. Put remaining butter in small saucepan. Add flour, salt, mustard, cinnamon, and ginger. Cook, stirring, 2–3 minutes. Remove from heat and pour on boiling orange juice, beating vigorously with a wire whisk. Cook, stirring, 5 minutes or until thickened. Pour over chicken and bake another 15 minutes. Set oven to broil and brown chicken for 2–3 minutes before serving.

Exchanges
3 Very Lean Meat
1 Fat

Calories 200
  Calories from Fat . . 55
Total Fat . . . . 6 g
  Saturated Fat . . . . . . 3 g
Cholesterol . . . . 81 mg
Sodium . . . . 359 mg
  W/o added salt . . . . 93 mg
Carbohydrate . . . . 7 g
  Dietary Fiber . . . . . . 0 g
  Sugars . . . . 5 g
Protein . . . . 27 g

Tomato, Chicken, and Cabbage Casserole

Serves 8   Serving Size: 1/8 recipe

  Boiling water to cover cabbage
3 cups shredded cabbage
1 onion, sliced
1 green bell pepper, chopped
1 Tbsp oil
1 lb tomatoes
  Nonfat cooking spray
2 cups cubed cooked chicken
3/4 cup dry bread crumbs
1/2 tsp granulated garlic
1/4 tsp pepper
1/2 tsp salt (optional)
1/4 cup grated Parmesan cheese
1 tsp oregano
1/4 tsp ground thyme
1 Tbsp melted butter

1. Preheat oven to 350°. Boil water in stockpot. Turn off heat, add cabbage, and blanch for 5 minutes. Drain and set aside.

2. Sauté onion and bell pepper in skillet in oil until onion is limp. Peel tomatoes and slice. Spray 3-quart casserole. Layer cabbage, onion mixture, tomatoes, and chicken in it.

3. Mix together the next 8 ingredients. Sprinkle over top of casserole. Bake 1 1/2 hours.

Exchanges
1/2 Starch   3 Lean Meat
1 Vegetable

Calories 230
  Calories from Fat . . 63
Total Fat . . . . 7 g
  Saturated Fat . . . . . . 2 g
Cholesterol . . . . 61 mg
Sodium . . . . 343 mg
  W/o added salt . . . 210 mg
Carbohydrate . . . . . . 16 g
  Dietary Fiber . . . . . . 2 g
  Sugars . . . . 6 g
Protein . . . . 25 g

Tamale Chicken Bake

Serves 6   Serving Size: 1/6 recipe

> 4 cups boiling water
> 1 cup cornmeal
> 1/2 tsp salt (optional)
> 2 Tbsp fresh or freeze-dried chives
>   Nonfat cooking spray
> 3 cups sliced cooked chicken
>   Salt (optional) and pepper to taste
> 1 15-oz can no-salt-added tomato sauce
> 1 10 1/2-oz pkg frozen corn, thawed
> 1 Tbsp sugar
> 1 Tbsp olive oil
> 1 Tbsp chopped fresh cilantro
> 1/2 cup raisins
> 1/4 cup sliced black olives
> 1/3 cup grated Parmesan cheese

1. Pour 3 cups boiling water into top of double boiler. Mix remaining one cup boiling water with cornmeal. Add salt. Add to water in top of double boiler very slowly, stirring constantly. Cover and cook 30 minutes, stirring occasionally over boiling water. Stir in chives.

2. Spray a 9 × 9 × 2-inch casserole. Add cornmeal and smooth the surface. Arrange chicken on cornmeal. Season to taste. Preheat oven to 350°.

3. Mix tomato sauce, corn, sugar, olive oil, cilantro, raisins, and black olives. Pour over chicken and sprinkle with Parmesan cheese. Bake 30 minutes.

Exchanges

3 Starch	2 Lean Meat
1 Vegetable	

Calories 373
  Calories from Fat . . 77
Total Fat . . . . 8 g
  Saturated Fat . . . . . . 2 g
Cholesterol . . . . 53 mg
Sodium . . . . 489 mg
  W/o added salt . . . 223 mg
Carbohydrate . . . . . . 51 g
  Dietary Fiber . . . . . . 5 g
  Sugars . . . . 16 g
Protein . . . . 26 g

Chicken Ring

Serves 8   Serving Size: 1/8 recipe

3 oz egg substitute
2 cups fat-free milk
2 whole eggs
1 cup soft bread crumbs
1/2 tsp salt (optional)
1 tsp Worcestershire sauce
3 cups cooked ground chicken
1/2 cup finely chopped celery
1 green bell pepper, finely chopped
1 pimiento, chopped
1 1/2 Tbsp lemon juice
3 green onions, chopped
Nonfat cooking spray
1/2 tsp paprika
1 lb mushrooms, sliced
1 Tbsp oil
Salt (optional) and pepper to taste

1. Preheat oven to 300°. Beat egg substitute with milk and whole eggs. Add next 9 ingredients and mix well.

2. Spray ring mold. Add egg-chicken mixture. Sprinkle with paprika. Place in pan in hot water that reaches halfway up the ring mold. Bake 50–60 minutes, or until a knife inserted in the middle comes out clean. Allow to rest 10 minutes.

3. Meanwhile, over medium-high heat, sauté mushrooms in oil 5 minutes, stirring often. Season. Place a serving plate over mold. Invert. Fill center of mold with mushrooms and serve. Or chill ring and fill with a salad of cooked navy beans, chopped onions, pimiento, oil, and vinegar.

Exchanges
1 Vegetable
3 Lean Meat

Calories 188
   Calories from Fat . . 45
Total Fat . . . . 5 g
   Saturated Fat . . . . . . 1 g
Cholesterol . . . . 86 mg
Sodium . . . . 332 mg
   W/o added salt . . . 132 mg
Carbohydrate . . . . . 103 g
   Dietary Fiber . . . . . . 1 g
   Sugars . . . . 4 g
Protein . . . . 26 g

Chicken Breasts Florentine

Serves 6 Serving Size: 1/6 recipe

> 3 Tbsp flour
>
> 1/2 tsp salt (optional)
>
> Freshly ground pepper
>
> 1/2 tsp nutmeg
>
> 3 boneless, skinless chicken breasts, halved
>
> 2 lb spinach or 1 lb broccoli florets
>
> Butter-flavored nonfat cooking spray
>
> 1 lb mushrooms, sliced
>
> 2 cups low-sodium chicken broth
>
> 3 Tbsp quick-mixing flour
>
> 1/2 cup fat-free or reduced-fat sour cream
>
> Salt (optional) and pepper to taste
>
> 1/2 tsp nutmeg
>
> 3 Tbsp grated Parmesan cheese

1. Mix flour, salt, pepper, and nutmeg. Roll chicken pieces in mixture. Wash spinach and put in pot. Cover and cook in the water on the leaves until they are wilted. Drain well. (If using broccoli, cook just until tender.)

2. Spray a nonstick skillet. Add mushrooms and cook, stirring constantly, 5 minutes. Remove. Spray skillet again. Add chicken breasts and brown on each side. Set aside.

3. Pour chicken broth into saucepan. Bring to the boil. Beat flour into sour cream. Remove pan from heat and beat mixture into broth. Place over heat and cook, stirring, until thickened. Season with salt, pepper, and nutmeg.

4. Place spinach in bottom of casserole. Mound around edges and shallow in the middle. Arrange mushrooms over spinach. Lay chicken pieces down middle. Spoon sauce over chicken. Sprinkle with cheese, place in oven, and bake 20 minutes.

Exchanges

3 Vegetable	4 Very Lean
1 Fat	Meat

Calories 261	
Calories from Fat . . 45	
Total Fat . . . . 5 g	
Saturated Fat . . . . . . 2 g	
Cholesterol . . . . 75 mg	
Sodium . . . . 541 mg	
W/o added salt . . . 274 mg	
Carbohydrate . . . . . . 17 g	
Dietary Fiber . . . . . . 5 g	
Sugars . . . . 2 g	
Protein . . . . 38 g	

Chicken Casserole with Herb Biscuits

Serves 8   Serving Size: 1/8 recipe

1	cup baby carrots
1	cup broccoli florets
3	leeks, well washed
1	Tbsp oil
1	cup chopped celery
1	onion, sliced
1	tsp basil
	Freshly ground pepper
1/2	tsp salt (optional)
5	dried shiitake mushrooms, soaked in hot water 30 minutes
2	cups strong chicken broth
1/2	cup quick-mixing flour
1 1/2	cups fat-free milk
1	Tbsp Worcestershire sauce
1/2	cup grated Parmesan cheese
1/2	cup chopped fresh parsley
3	cups cubed cooked chicken
	Biscuits (next recipe)

1. Steam carrots and broccoli until tender. Drain and set aside. Cut white part of leeks into 1/4-inch pieces. Heat nonstick skillet and add oil. Over medium-high heat, sauté leeks 5 minutes. Add celery and onion. Cook until onion is limp. Sprinkle with basil, pepper, and salt. Drain mushrooms, reserving liquid. Chop and add to leek mixture. Sauté 2–3 minutes.

2. Add mushroom liquid to broth. Pour into saucepan. Stir in flour and beat with wire whisk until smooth. Add milk. Cook, stirring, until it thickens. Add Worcestershire, cheese, and parsley.

3. Preheat oven to 400°. Place vegetables in casserole. Scatter leek mixture over all. Cover with chicken. Pour sauce over all. Make biscuits, below, and place on top of casserole. Bake, uncovered, for 25 minutes.

Exchanges

1 Starch	3 Lean Meat
1 Vegetable	

Calories 360
  Calories from Fat . . 63
Total Fat . . . . 7 g
  Saturated Fat . . . . . . 2 g
Cholesterol . . . . 60 mg
Sodium . . . . 387 mg
  W/o added salt . . . 254 mg
Carbohydrate . . . . . . 22 g
  Dietary Fiber . . . . . . 3 g
  Sugars . . . . 6 g
Protein . . . . 28 g

Herb Biscuits

These biscuits can be baked on top of the casserole or separately.

Serves 8   Serving Size: 1 biscuit

> 2 cups flour
> 2 tsp baking powder
> 1/2 tsp baking soda
> 1 tsp salt (optional)
> 1 tsp oregano
> 1 tsp dried chives or 1 Tbsp fresh
> 4 Tbsp margarine
> 1 egg yolk
> 8 oz plain yogurt
> 1 egg white beaten with 1 Tbsp water

1. Mix flour, baking powder, soda, salt, oregano, and chives in bowl. Add margarine and blend until crumbly. Add egg yolk and yogurt. Blend until dough leaves the sides of the bowl.

2. Turn onto floured surface and knead several times. You can drop mixture on top of casserole by spoon or roll into a flat 1-inch thick disc and cut 8 biscuits, using a 2-inch cookie cutter or glass. Place on top of casserole and brush with egg white wash. Bake in 400° oven, uncovered, for 25 minutes. These biscuits may also be placed on a baking sheet that has been sprayed with cooking spray and baked 15–20 minutes.

Exchanges
2 Starch
1/2 Fat

Calories 191
　Calories from Fat . . 63
Total Fat . . . . 7 g
　Saturated Fat . . . . . . 1 g
Cholesterol . . . . 27 mg
Sodium . . . . 444 mg
　W/o added salt . . . 177 mg
Carbohydrate . . . . . . 28 g
　Dietary Fiber . . . . . . 1 g
　Sugars . . . . 1 g
Protein . . . . 6 g

Chicken Marsala

Serves 6   Serving Size: 1/6 recipe

> 3 boneless, skinless chicken breasts, halved
> Flour for dredging
> 2 Tbsp butter
> 3 Tbsp Marsala wine
> 1 Tbsp flour
> 1 cup low-sodium chicken broth, boiling
> 1 tsp flour
> 1/4 cup fat-free or reduced-fat sour cream
> Salt (optional) and pepper to taste
> 1 tsp currant jelly
> 1 Tbsp grated Parmesan cheese

1. Preheat oven to 350°. Dust chicken breasts with flour. Over medium-high heat, melt 1 Tbsp butter in nonstick skillet. Brown breasts on each side. Pour wine over all and cook until evaporated. Remove chicken.

2. Add remaining butter to skillet. Stir in 1 Tbsp flour. Cook, stirring, 1–2 minutes. Remove from heat and pour on boiling broth, beating with wire whisk to prevent lumping. Return to heat and cook 5 minutes to thicken. Add 1 tsp flour to sour cream and beat well. Beat into sauce. Add salt, pepper, and jelly. Heat to melt jelly.

3. Place chicken breasts in casserole. Pour sauce over all, sprinkle with Parmesan, and bake for 15 minutes. If not brown enough, run under broiler 1–2 minutes before serving.

Exchanges

1/2 Carbohydrate
4 Very Lean Meat
1 Fat

Calories 230
  Calories from Fat . . 63
Total Fat . . . . 7 g
  Saturated Fat . . . . . . 3 g
Cholesterol . . . . 84 mg
Sodium . . . . 224 mg
  W/o added salt . . . 135 mg
Carbohydrate . . . . 7 g
  Dietary Fiber . . . . . . 0 g
  Sugars . . . . 1 g
Protein . . . . 30 g

Ethnic Dishes

Here are twelve chicken dishes with a distinct foreign flavor, typical of the cuisine found in these countries. They have been adapted to be healthier than the original versions and still retain their unique qualities.

Argentinean Orange Chicken

Serves 8   Serving Size: 1/8 recipe

2 (3 lb) chickens, cut in pieces, skin removed
Nonfat cooking spray
Salt (optional) and pepper to taste
1 cup low-sodium chicken broth
1 cup orange juice
Zest of 1 orange, grated
2 Tbsp cornstarch
2 Tbsp red wine (Argentinean if available)
2 Tbsp chopped fresh parsley

1. Heat broiler. Spray tray with cooking spray and lay chicken pieces on it. Sprinkle with salt and pepper, and broil on each side until browned, about 15 minutes. Remove chicken and place in 9 × 12-inch casserole, thighs and legs on bottom, breasts on top. Set oven to 350°.

2. Mix broth, orange juice, and zest. Pour over chicken. Bake, covered, 30 minutes. Remove chicken from liquids and keep warm. Skim fat from liquids and discard.

3. Place liquids over low heat on top of stove. Mix cornstarch with red wine. Pour into liquids and cook, stirring, until thickened and clear. Place chicken on a heated platter. Pour sauce over all and sprinkle with parsley.

Exchanges
4 Lean Meat

Calories 221
  Calories from Fat . . 70
Total Fat . . . . 8 g
  Saturated Fat . . . . . . 2 g
Cholesterol . . . . 90 mg
Sodium . . . . 165 mg
  W/o added salt . . . . .98 mg
Carbohydrate . . . . 6 g
  Dietary Fiber . . . . . . 0 g
  Sugars . . . . 3 g
Protein . . . . 30 g

Croque Madame — Canada

In French Canada, these elegant luncheon sandwiches are served with maple syrup.

Serves 4   Serving Size: 1 sandwich

  8 slices white, homemade-style bread
  4 tsp butter, soft
  4 thin slices cooked chicken breast
  4 thin slices low-salt, reduced-fat Swiss cheese
    Salt (optional) and pepper to taste
  8 oz egg substitute
1/4 cup fat-free milk
    Nonfat cooking spray

1. Spread each of 4 slices of bread with 1 tsp butter. Top with a slice of chicken and a slice of cheese. Place remaining slices of bread on top of each sandwich. Skewer with toothpicks.

2. Beat egg substitute with 1/4 cup of milk. Dip each sandwich in batter, covering well. Heavily spray a nonstick skillet. Sauté sandwiches on each side until golden brown, 5–7 minutes total. Cut each sandwich in half diagonally and serve two halves per person.

Exchanges
2 Starch   1 Fat
3 Very Lean Meat

Calories 239
  Calories from Fat . . 72
Total Fat . . . . 8 g
  Saturated Fat . . . . . . 4 g
Cholesterol . . . . 52 mg
Sodium . . . . 563 mg
  W/o added salt . . . 296 mg
Carbohydrate . . . . 4 g
  Dietary Fiber . . . . . . 1 g
  Sugars . . . . 2 g
Protein . . . . 25 g

Kota Kapama or Greek Braised Chicken with Cinnamon

Serves 4   Serving Size: 1/4 recipe

Nonfat cooking spray
1 large onion, chopped
3 cloves garlic, crushed
6 ripe tomatoes, peeled, seeded, chopped
2 Tbsp no-salt-added tomato paste
1/2 cup low-sodium chicken broth
1/2 tsp cinnamon
1/2 tsp salt (optional)
Freshly ground pepper to taste
Nonfat cooking spray
2 boneless, skinless chicken breasts, halved
1/4 cup grated Parmesan cheese

1. Spray 2-quart pot with cooking spray. Add onion and sauté, stirring, until limp. Add garlic and sauté 1 minute over medium-high heat. Add tomatoes, tomato paste, broth, cinnamon, salt, and pepper. Mix well. Simmer, covered, 30 minutes. If too thick, add a little chicken broth.

2. Heat broiler. Spray broiler tray. Add chicken breasts and brown quickly on all sides, about 5 minutes. Turn oven to 350°. Place browned chicken in casserole. Pour sauce over all and sprinkle with cheese. Bake, uncovered, 20 minutes.

Exchanges

3 Vegetable   1/2 Fat
4 Very Lean Meat

Calories 247
  Calories from Fat . . 45
Total Fat . . . . 5 g
  Saturated Fat . . . . . . 2 g
Cholesterol . . . . 78 mg
Sodium . . . . 485 mg
  W/o added salt . . . 218 mg
Carbohydrate . . . . . . 14 g
  Dietary Fiber . . . . . . 2 g
  Sugars . . . . 6 g
Protein . . . . 34 g

Greek Orzo Chicken Salad

Serves 6   Serving Size: 1/6 recipe

    1 lb orzo macaroni
    1 Tbsp olive oil
    1 Tbsp lemon juice
    1 clove garlic, crushed
    1 tsp salt (optional)
       Freshly ground pepper
    1 Tbsp chopped fresh dill
  1/2 Spanish onion, finely chopped
  1/2 cup chopped pitted kalamata olives
    2 cups chopped cooked chicken
    1 cup crumbled feta cheese
    1 head Boston lettuce, well washed and drained

1. Put orzo into 1 gallon of boiling water and cook, stirring occasionally, until al dente or barely tender. Drain well and place in a large bowl. Mix oil, lemon juice, garlic, salt, pepper, and dill. Pour over warm orzo. Mix well, then cool. Carefully mix in the onion, olives, chicken, and feta cheese.

2. Separate 6 whole unblemished leaves from the lettuce. Place on 6 individual salad plates. Mound salad on each leaf, dividing total recipe equally.

Exchanges

4 Starch	4 Lean Meat
1/2 Fat	

Calories 563
   Calories from Fat . . 171
Total Fat . . . . 19 g
   Saturated Fat . . . . . . 8 g
Cholesterol . . . . 86 mg
Sodium . . . . 1,248 mg
   W/o added salt . . . 523 mg
Carbohydrate . . . . . . 57 g
   Dietary Fiber . . . . . . 4 g
   Sugars . . . . 4 g
Protein . . . . 40 g

Chicken Cacciatore

Serves 6   Serving Size: 1/6 recipe

> 1 (3–4 lb) chicken, cut in pieces, skin removed
> Salt (optional) and freshly ground pepper
> Nonfat cooking spray
> 1/2 lb mushrooms, sliced
> 1 onion, sliced
> 2 small carrots, cut in strips
> 1 clove garlic, crushed
> 1/2 cup white wine
> 1 28-oz can no-salt-added crushed tomatoes
> 1/2 yellow bell pepper, sliced
> 1 tsp rosemary, crushed
> 1/2 cup low-sodium chicken broth
> 2 Tbsp grated Parmesan cheese

1. Wash chicken. Salt and pepper to taste. Heat broiler. Spray broiler tray and broil chicken pieces quickly on each side, about 5–7 minutes total. Set aside.

2. Spray a nonstick skillet. Add mushrooms and sauté over medium-high heat, stirring, 5 minutes. Set aside. Again spray skillet and sauté onion and carrots until onion is limp. Add garlic and sauté 1 minute. Pour wine over this and reduce over high heat until 2–3 Tbsp remain. Add tomatoes, bell pepper, rosemary, and broth. Cook 5 minutes. Preheat the oven to 350°.

3. Place chicken in casserole with lid. Scatter mushrooms over top. Pour tomato sauce over all. Cover and bake 45 minutes or until chicken is tender. Sprinkle with Parmesan cheese before serving.

Exchanges
4 Vegetable
4 Lean Meat

Calories 290
  Calories from Fat . . 72
Total Fat . . . . 8 g
  Saturated Fat . . . . . . 2 g
Cholesterol . . . . 60 mg
Sodium . . . . 521 mg
  W/o added salt . . . 432 mg
Carbohydrate . . . . . . 21 g
  Dietary Fiber . . . . . . 3 g
  Sugars . . . . 9 g
Protein . . . . 32 g

Chicken Polenta Pie

Serves 6   Serving Size: 1/6 recipe

  Nonfat cooking spray
1 small onion, chopped
1 cup sliced mushrooms
1 clove garlic, crushed
1 28-oz can no-salt-added crushed tomatoes
2 Tbsp tomato paste
1 tsp oregano
1/2 tsp basil
1/2 tsp marjoram
1 bay leaf
  Freshly ground pepper
1 boneless, skinless chicken breast, chopped
2/3 cup cornmeal or polenta
1 cup cold water
1/2 tsp salt (optional)
1/4 cup grated Parmesan cheese
1 10-oz pkg chopped frozen spinach, thawed, well drained
1/2 cup grated Telegio or Fontina cheese

1. Spray a large nonstick skillet. Add onion and cook over medium-high heat until limp. Spray again and add mushrooms. Cook 5 minutes, stirring. Add garlic and cook 1 minute. Add tomatoes, tomato paste, oregano, basil, marjoram, bay leaf, and pepper. Bring to the boil, cover and simmer 30 minutes. Uncover, add chicken and cook another 10 minutes, stirring occasionally, until thick and chicken is no longer pink. Discard bay leaf.

2. Meanwhile, bring 1 1/2 cups water to the boil. Mix cornmeal or polenta, cold water, and salt. Slowly stir it into the boiling water. When mixture returns to a boil, reduce heat to simmer, and cook 15 minutes, stirring occasionally. When very thick, stir in Parmesan cheese.

3. Preheat oven to 350°. Spray 9 × 11 × 2-inch baking dish well. Spread 1/2 the cornmeal/polenta mixture in bottom of dish. Arrange spinach over this. Spoon chicken mixture over all. Layer remaining cornmeal/polenta mixture over top. Sprinkle with grated cheese. Bake until cheese is melted and pie is heated through.

Exchanges

1 Starch	3 Lean Meat
1 Vegetable	

Calories 360
  Calories from Fat . . 63
Total Fat . . . . 7 g
  Saturated Fat . . . . . . 2 g
Cholesterol . . . . 60 mg
Sodium . . . . 387 mg
  W/o added salt . . . 254 mg
Carbohydrate . . . . . . 22 g
  Dietary Fiber . . . . . . 3 g
  Sugars . . . . 6 g
Protein . . . . 28 g

Chicken Sukiyaki

In Japan sukiyaki is cooked at the table and served with individual bowls of sushi rice. You can do this using an electric wok or frying pan.

Serves 6   Serving Size: 1/6 of recipe

Nonfat cooking spray
1 boneless, skinless chicken breast, cut in thin strips
2 cups sliced mushrooms (shiitake)
1/2 cup peeled and diced butternut squash
1/2 cup lite soy sauce
1/2 cup honey
1/4 cup sherry
1 cup water
1 small zucchini, cut in 1/4-inch pieces
3 cups chopped kale or mustard greens
4 green onions, cut into 2-inch lengths
2 cups bean sprouts
1 tsp grated fresh ginger

1. Spray large electric skillet or wok with cooking spray. Sauté chicken over high heat until no longer pink, about 5 minutes. Remove if using skillet, or push to one side if using wok.

2. Spray, add mushrooms, and cook 5 minutes. Remove or push aside. Spray and add squash. Mix soy sauce, honey, sherry, and 1/2 cup water and pour over squash. Bring to the boil, lower heat, and cook until tender.

3. Spray and add zucchini, kale, green onions, and bean sprouts. If too dry, add a little water. Cook 5 minutes. Add ginger and toss well. Cook 1 minute. Spray and add chicken and mushrooms. Mix well. Serve from the wok or frying pan.

Exchanges
2 Vegetable
1 Carbohydrate
1 Very Lean Meat

Calories 221
  Calories from Fat . . 15
Total Fat . . . . 2 g
  Saturated Fat . . . . . . 0 g
Cholesterol . . . . 24 mg
Sodium . . . . 851 mg
Carbohydrate . . . . . . 36 g
  Dietary Fiber . . . . . . 4 g
  Sugars . . . . 27 g
Protein . . . . 15 g

Stuffed Mexican Chicken Breasts

This is a truly delicious dish, but rather peppery. Anaheim chilis are very mild, but flavorful, while jalapeños are hot. If hot is not your thing, don't use the jalapeños.

Serves 4   Serving Size: 1/4 recipe

- 1 small zucchini, grated
- 1 small crookneck squash, grated
- 2 Anaheim chili peppers
- Nonfat cooking spray
- 2 boneless, skinless chicken breasts, halved
- 2 green onions, chopped
- 1 Tbsp chopped jalapeño peppers
- 1/2 tsp oregano
- 1/2 tsp cumin
- 4 tsp grated Parmesan cheese
- 1 1/4 cup low-sodium chicken broth
- 1/2 cup fat-free or reduced-fat sour cream

1. Preheat oven to 425°. Place zucchini and squash in a clean cloth and roll tightly to squeeze out liquids. Cut Anaheim peppers in half. Remove stems, seeds, and membranes. Spray baking sheet. Lay chilies, cut side down, on tray. Bake 20 minutes, or until peppers have blistered and turned dark. Place peppers in brown paper bag for 30 minutes. Rub skins off under running water. Chop and set aside.

2. Slash a pocket in each chicken breast. Spray a deep nonstick skillet with cooking spray. Add green onions, zucchini, squash, jalapeños, and half the Anaheim peppers. Cook over medium-high heat, stirring, for 5–6 minutes. Add oregano and cumin. Cool. Stuff breasts with mixture. Sprinkle 1 tsp Parmesan cheese on each breast. Close with toothpicks.

3. Heat skillet and spray. Brown chicken breasts. Pour broth over chicken, add remaining Anaheim peppers. Cover and simmer 10 minutes. Remove breasts and keep warm. Reduce liquids over high heat until 1/4 cup remains. Beat in sour cream. Remove toothpicks from chicken. Serve each with a spoonful of sauce.

Exchanges

1 Vegetable
1/2 Carbohydrate
4 Very Lean Meat

Calories 217
   Calories from Fat . . 36
Total Fat . . . . 4 g
   Saturated Fat . . . . . . 1 g
Cholesterol . . . . 75 mg
Sodium . . . . 173 mg
Carbohydrate . . . . . . 11 g
   Dietary Fiber . . . . . . 3 g
   Sugars . . . . 3 g
Protein . . . . 33 g

Mexican
Chicken Enchiladas

If you like really peppery foods, use 1/2 cup of chopped jalapeños. If your taste is cooler, use 1/4 cup. This will be hot, but not hair raising.

Serves 6 Serving Size: 1/6 recipe

1	boneless, skinless chicken breast
1/2	lb fresh spinach, washed and chopped
2	green onions, finely chopped
1	cup fat-free sour cream
2	Tbsp quick-mixing flour
1/2	tsp ground cumin
	Freshly ground pepper
1/2	tsp salt (optional)
1/4–1/2	cup chopped jalapeño peppers
6	flour tortillas
	Nonfat cooking spray
1	cup fat-free milk
1/2	cup shredded reduced-fat, reduced-salt Monterey Jack cheese
	Bunch green onions, cleaned and chopped
	Salsa, below

1. Place chicken in a 3-quart saucepan. Cover with water and bring to boil. Reduce heat and simmer 15 minutes. Drain and cool. Chop and set aside. Place spinach in saucepan, cover, and cook for 5 minutes or until wilted. Drain. Press out excess liquid and set aside.

2. Mix chicken and green onions. Add spinach and mix well. Combine sour cream, flour, cumin, pepper, and salt. Stir in jalapeños. Mix half this sauce with chicken mixture. Divide equally between 6 tortillas and roll to enclose filling. Spray shallow baking dish and lay enchiladas seam side down in it. Preheat oven to 350°.

3. Stir milk into remaining sauce. Pour over enchiladas, sprinkle with cheese, and bake for 20–25 minutes. Transfer to warm serving platter. Sprinkle with green onions and serve with salsa, below.

Exchanges
2 Starch
2 Lean Meat

Calories 275
   Calories from Fat . . 63
Total Fat . . . . 7 g
   Saturated Fat . . . . . . 3 g
Cholesterol . . . . 38 mg
Sodium . . . . 670 mg
   W/o added salt . . . 942 mg
Carbohydrate . . . . . . 29 g
   Dietary Fiber . . . . . . 1 g
   Sugars . . . . 2 g
Protein . . . . 23 g

Salsa

Serves 8   Serving Size: 2 Tbsp

2 tomatoes

Nonfat cooking spray

1 clove garlic, crushed

1/2–1 Tbsp canned chopped jalapeños

1 Tbsp chopped fresh parsley

1/2 cup low-sodium chicken broth

1 1/2 Tbsp olive oil

1/2 onion, minced

1 tsp oregano

1. Preheat oven to 350°. Spray tomatoes with cooking spray. Place in oven and bake 20 minutes. Cool, peel, remove seeds, and chop. Place in a small saucepan. Add garlic, jalapeños, parsley, broth, and olive oil. Bring to a boil, cover, and simmer 10 minutes. Stir in onions and oregano. Cool. Makes 2 cups

Exchanges
1/2 Fat

Calories 24
Calories from Fat . . 18
Total Fat . . . . 2 g
Saturated Fat . . . . . . 0 g
Cholesterol . . . . 0 mg
Sodium . . . . 17 mg
Carbohydrate . . . . 2 g
Dietary Fiber . . . . . . 0 g
Sugars . . . . 0 g
Protein . . . . 0 g

Chicken Chili

Serves 10   Serving Size: 1/10 recipe

1 Tbsp canola oil

1 onion, chopped

1 clove garlic, crushed

3 cups finely chopped cooked chicken

4 cups low-sodium chicken broth

1 28-oz can no-salt-added crushed tomatoes

1 15 1/2-oz can pinto beans, rinsed and drained

1 15-oz can black beans, rinsed and drained

1 4-oz can chopped jalapeño peppers, drained
  (2 oz for less heat)

1 Tbsp chili powder

1 Tbsp ground cumin

1 tsp salt (optional)

Freshly ground pepper

1. Over medium-high heat, heat the oil in a large pot. Add onion and cook until limp, about 5 minutes. Add garlic and cook, stirring, 1 minute. Add all remaining ingredients and bring to a boil. Reduce heat and simmer, stirring occasionally, until thickened (approximately 50–60 minutes).

Exchanges

1 Starch	2 Lean Meat
1 Vegetable	

Calories 236
  Calories from Fat . . 36
Total Fat . . . . 4 g
  Saturated Fat . . . . . . 1 g
Cholesterol . . . . 44 mg
Sodium . . . . 818 mg
  W/o added salt . . . 605 mg
Carbohydrate . . . . . . 24 g
  Dietary Fiber . . . . . . 3 g
  Sugars . . . . 2 g
Protein . . . . 24 g

Spanish Paella

You may find the saffron too expensive, so leave it out. The rice will not have that lovely orange color, but the dish will stand very well on its own.

Serves 8   Serving Size: 1/8 recipe

- 1 lb mussels
- Nonfat cooking spray
- 1 (4 lb) chicken, cut in pieces, skin removed
- 1 onion, chopped
- 1 green bell pepper, seeded, cut in strips
- 1 clove garlic, crushed
- Salt (optional) and freshly ground pepper
- 1 cup rice
- 2 tomatoes, peeled, seeded, chopped
- 2 cups low-sodium chicken broth
- Large pinch saffron, soaked in 3 Tbsp hot water for 20–30 minutes (optional)
- 1/2 lb chorizo or Italian sausage
- 1 10 1/2-oz pkg frozen peas

1. Scrub mussels and remove beards. Heat broiler. Spray broiler tray. Brown chicken pieces on all sides for about 7–8 minutes total. Set aside.

2. Heat large nonstick skillet. Spray. Add onion and cook over medium-high heat, stirring, until limp. Add green bell pepper and garlic. Season to taste and cook 5 minutes, stirring. Remove with slotted spoon. Spray again. Add rice and cook, stirring, 5 minutes. Add tomatoes, broth, and saffron (optional). Stir well. Bring to the boil.

3. Place chicken and vegetables on top of rice. Simmer uncovered on top of the stove until liquid has been partially absorbed. Meanwhile, slice sausage and brown in nonstick skillet. Drain fat and add sausage to paella. Cook until most liquid is absorbed. Add mussels and peas. Cook until mussels open. Cook until all liquid is absorbed. Discard any mussels that do not open. If rice is not soft, add a small amount of chicken broth and cook until absorbed.

Exchanges

1 Starch	3 Lean Meat
1 Vegetable	

Calories 360
  Calories from Fat . . 63
Total Fat . . . . 7 g
  Saturated Fat . . . . . . 2 g
Cholesterol . . . . 60 mg
Sodium . . . . 387 mg
  W/o added salt . . . 254 mg
Carbohydrate . . . . . . 22 g
  Dietary Fiber . . . . . . 3 g
  Sugars . . . . 6 g
Protein . . . . 28 g

Spanish Tortilla

Serves 8   Serving Size: 1/8 recipe

Nonfat cooking spray
1 small potato, peeled, very thinly sliced
1 small onion, chopped
1/2 red bell pepper, chopped
3 green onions, chopped
1 cup cooked ground chicken
4 eggs, beaten
8 oz egg substitute
1 tsp oregano
Pinch ground thyme
1/2 tsp salt (optional)
Freshly ground pepper
1/2 cup grated Parmesan cheese

1. Spray large nonstick skillet. Arrange potato slices over surface of skillet. Cook 3–4 minutes over low heat. Turn, spraying under potatoes again. Cook 3–4 minutes. Spray another skillet and sauté onion, bell pepper, and green onions over medium-high heat until onion is limp. Scatter over potatoes. Scatter chicken over potatoes.

2. Beat eggs, egg substitute, oregano, and thyme together. Add salt and pepper. Pour over potato mixture. Let eggs cook over low heat, lifting edges to allow egg batter to flow underneath. When all mixture has set and surface is still moist, sprinkle with cheese. Cover and let stand, over very low heat, until cheese has melted. Cut into portions and serve warm or at room temperature. You may add leftover vegetables to the tortilla just before adding the egg mixture.

Exchanges
3 Lean Meat

Calories 166
  Calories from Fat . . 54
Total Fat . . . . 6 g
  Saturated Fat . . . . . . 2 g
Cholesterol . . . . 140 mg
Sodium . . . . 352 mg
  W/o added salt . . . 219 mg
Carbohydrate . . . . 5 g
  Dietary Fiber . . . . . . 1 g
  Sugars . . . . 1 g
Protein . . . . 22 g

Chicken and Fruit Combinations

Fruit and chicken have a natural affinity for each other. One seems to enhance and compliment the flavor of the other. This is not a large category, but a truly delicious one. Most of these recipes lend themselves admirably to entertaining.

Chicken Medallions
with Dried Fruit in Phyllo

Serves 8   Serving Size: 1 bundle

>   2 boneless, skinless chicken breasts, halved
>   1/2 cup chopped dried apricots
>   1/2 cup finely chopped pecans
>   1/2 cup plain yogurt
>   1/2 tsp nutmeg
>   Pinch ground thyme
>   1/2 tsp salt (optional)
>   Freshly ground pepper
>   8 sheets phyllo pastry
>   Nonfat cooking spray

1. Preheat oven to 400°. Place each chicken breast half between 2 sheets wax paper or plastic wrap. Tap with wooden mallet until 1/4 inch thick. Cut in half. Again tap with wooden mallet to even out. Mix apricots, pecans, yogurt, nutmeg, thyme, salt, and pepper. Spread evenly over each chicken medallion. Fold in half.

2. Lay one sheet of phyllo on a board. Spray well. Fold in half and spray again. Fold in half again and spray.

3. Place one chicken medallion in the center and fold phyllo around it to form a little bundle. Place bundle seam side down on sprayed baking sheet. Repeat until all chicken is wrapped. Spray bundles before placing in oven. Bake 30 minutes or until golden brown.

Exchanges

1 Starch	1 Fat
2 Very Lean Meat	

Calories 202
   Calories from Fat . . 63
Total Fat . . . . 7 g
   Saturated Fat . . . . . . 1 g
Cholesterol . . . . 37 mg
Sodium . . . . 266 mg
   W/o added salt . . . 132 mg
Carbohydrate . . . . . . 17 g
   Dietary Fiber . . . . . . 1 g
   Sugars . . . . 4 g
Protein . . . . 17 g

Chicken Wing Drumsticks
with Pear Dipping Sauce

Serves 12   Serving Size: 3 pieces

      3 lb chicken wings
         Nonfat cooking spray
    1/2 tsp salt (optional)
         Freshly ground pepper
      1 tsp granulated garlic
         Juice 1 lemon
      4 ripe pears, peeled
      2 Tbsp brown sugar
    1/4 tsp each cinnamon, nutmeg, and ground ginger
         Freshly ground pepper
    1/8 tsp salt
      3 Tbsp sherry
         Dash hot pepper sauce

1. Preheat oven to 375°. Cut each chicken wing at drumstick joint and use wing for making broth. Strip skin from each "drumstick." Spray baking sheet and lay drumsticks on sheet. Spray them with cooking spray. Sprinkle with salt, pepper, and garlic. Squeeze lemon juice over all. Bake 25–30 minutes or until browned and crispy.

2. Place pears in saucepan. Mash with potato masher. Over low heat, cook to extract juice (about 15 minutes). Add sugar, lemon juice, and seasonings, and cook until thickened. Stir often to prevent scorching. Add sherry and hot pepper sauce. Puree in food processor or blender.

Exchanges
1 Fruit
2 Very Lean Meat

Calories 138
   Calories from Fat . . 36
Total Fat . . . . 4 g
   Saturated Fat . . . . . . 1 g
Cholesterol . . . . 44 mg
Sodium . . . . 155 mg
   W/o added salt . . . . 45 mg
Carbohydrate . . . . . . 12 g
   Dietary Fiber . . . . . . 2 g
   Sugars . . . . 6 g
Protein . . . . 13 g

Sautéed Chicken Breasts with Nectarines and Pistachio Nuts

Serves 4   Serving Size: 1/4 recipe

> 1 1/2 cups pear nectar
> 1/2 tsp cinnamon
> Juice 1 lemon
> 2 nectarines, unpeeled, pitted, chopped
> 1 Tbsp brown sugar
> 1 Tbsp cornstarch
> 2 Tbsp sherry
> 2 boneless, skinless chicken breasts, halved
> Salt (optional) and freshly ground pepper
> Nonfat cooking spray
> 1/2 cup dry white wine
> 1/2 cup finely chopped pistachio nuts

1. Place first 5 ingredients in small saucepan. Bring to boil, and simmer 10–15 minutes. Put into a blender or food processor and puree. Return to heat and bring to a boil. Mix cornstarch with sherry. Stir into sauce and cook until clear and thickened.

2. Season chicken breasts with salt and pepper. Heat and spray nonstick skillet with cooking spray. Add chicken breasts and sauté over low heat until browned. Add wine, cover and cook 15 minutes, or until they resist the pressure of a finger. Place breasts on a heated platter. Pour sauce over all, then sprinkle with pistachio nuts, or serve sauce and nuts on the side.

Exchanges

2 Fruit	2 Fat
4 Very Lean Meat	

Calories 380
    Calories from Fat . . 99
Total Fat . . . . 11 g
    Saturated Fat . . . . . . 2 g
Cholesterol . . . . 73 mg
Sodium . . . . 200 mg
    W/o added salt . . . . 67 mg
Carbohydrate . . . . . . 34 g
    Dietary Fiber . . . . . . 3 g
    Sugars . . . . 8 g
Protein . . . . 32 g

Quick and Easy Orange-Glazed Chicken

Serves 4   Serving Size: 1/4 recipe

      Nonfat cooking spray

2 boneless, skinless chicken breasts, halved

1/2 cup 100%-fruit orange marmalade

1 tsp rosemary

1/2 tsp ground cloves

1/2 tsp lemon pepper marinade

1 tsp garlic powder

1 Tbsp lemon juice

1 Tbsp chopped fresh mint, or 1 tsp dried

      Salt (optional) and freshly ground pepper

1. Preheat oven to 350°. Spray nonstick skillet. Cook chicken breasts over medium heat and brown on each side. Remove and place in sprayed shallow baking dish.

2. Mix marmalade with rosemary, cloves, lemon pepper marinade, garlic powder, lemon juice, and mint. Heat, stirring, until marmalade melts.

3. Season chicken breasts with salt and pepper. Brush with marmalade mixture. Bake 10 minutes. Turn breasts and brush with marmalade mixture. Bake another 8–10 minutes. Brush with marmalade glaze just before serving.

Exchanges
3 Very Lean Meat

Calories 252
   Calories from Fat . . 30
Total Fat . . . . 3 g
   Saturated Fat . . . . . . 1 g
Cholesterol . . . . 73 mg
Sodium . . . . 203 mg
   W/o added salt . . . . 70 mg
Carbohydrate . . . . . . 28 g
   Dietary Fiber . . . . . . 2 g
   Sugars . . . . 0 g
Protein . . . . 27 g

Chicken with Green Grapes

Serves 6   Serving Size: 1/6 recipe

3 boneless, skinless chicken breasts, halved
1/2 tsp salt (optional)
1/2 tsp nutmeg
   Freshly ground pepper
1 Tbsp olive oil
1 Tbsp apricot jam
1/2 tsp tarragon
4 green onions, chopped
1/2 cup dry white wine
1 cup seedless green grapes
1/4 cup evaporated fat-free milk

1. Sprinkle chicken with salt, nutmeg, and pepper. In large nonstick skillet, heat oil. Brown chicken breasts on each side.

2. Add jam, tarragon, green onions, and wine. Cover, reduce heat to simmer, and cook 15 minutes. Add grapes and cook 5 minutes. Remove chicken and grapes with slotted spoon and keep warm.

1. Add milk to the pan. Turn heat up and reduce, uncovered, until liquids thicken. Spoon over chicken and grapes and serve.

Exchanges

1/2 Carbohydrate   1/2 Fat
4 Very Lean Meat

Calories 207
   Calories from Fat . . 45
Total Fat . . . . 5 g
   Saturated Fat . . . . . . 1 g
Cholesterol . . . . 73 mg
Sodium . . . . 251 mg
   W/o added salt . . . . 73 mg
Carbohydrate . . . . 6 g
   Dietary Fiber . . . . . . 0 g
   Sugars . . . . 3 g
Protein . . . . 29 g

Chicken with Figs

Serves 4   Serving Size: 1/4 recipe

4	dried figs, quartered and chopped
2	Tbsp dry sherry
1/2	cup flour
1/2	tsp salt (optional)
1/4	tsp white pepper
1	Tbsp olive oil
2	boneless, skinless chicken breasts, halved
2	cloves garlic, crushed
1	onion, thinly sliced
1/2	small green bell pepper, chopped
1	tomato, peeled, seeded, chopped
1/2	tsp salt (optional)
	Freshly ground pepper
1/2	tsp cinnamon
1/2	cup low-sodium chicken broth
1/4	cup finely chopped walnuts

1. Place figs in a small bowl. Pour sherry over and marinate 15 minutes.

2. Mix flour, salt, and pepper. Roll chicken in flour mixture. Heat oil in large, nonstick skillet. Sauté chicken breasts until golden on each side. Remove from skillet.

3. Add garlic, onion, and green bell pepper. Cook until onion is limp. Add fig mixture, tomato, salt, pepper, and cinnamon. Return chicken to skillet. Bring to the boil. Cover and cook 3–4 minutes. Add broth, cover, and cook another 8 minutes, or until chicken is tender. Place chicken on heated platter. Pour vegetable-fig sauce over all. Sprinkle with chopped walnuts and serve. Or serve sauce and nuts on the side.

Exchanges
1 1/2 Carbohydrate   1 Fat
3 Very Lean Meat

Calories	298
Calories from Fat . .	90
Total Fat	10 g
Saturated Fat	1.5 g
Cholesterol	73 mg
Sodium	410 mg
W/o added salt	79 mg
Carbohydrate	20 g
Dietary Fiber	4 g
Sugars	6 g
Protein	30 g

Hawaiian Chicken

Serves 6   Serving Size: 1/6 recipe

1 star fruit

3 Tbsp honey

1 28-oz can pineapple slices

3 boneless, skinless chicken breasts, halved

1 tsp granulated garlic

Salt (optional) and pepper

1 Tbsp canola oil

1 Tbsp grated fresh ginger

1 Tbsp lite soy sauce

2 Tbsp sherry

1 Tbsp cornstarch

Grated rind 1 lime

1. Cut a very thin strip from each edge of star fruit ribs and discard. Slice star fruit into 1/4-inch pieces. Remove pits. Place in small bowl and pour honey over all. Drain pineapple rings, reserving juice.

2. Wash chicken breasts. Sprinkle with garlic, salt, and pepper. Heat oil in large nonstick skillet. Brown chicken breasts over medium-high heat. Sprinkle with ginger, and add 1/2 cup pineapple juice. Cover and cook over medium-low heat for 5 minutes.

3. Add six pineapple slices. Mix star fruit, remaining pineapple juice, and soy sauce. Pour over chicken, cover, and cook 5 minutes. Mix sherry with cornstarch. Pour into liquids in skillet and cook until clear and thickened, about 3 minutes.

4. Arrange chicken on platter. Arrange pineapple and star fruit over chicken. Pour sauce over all and sprinkle with lime zest.

Exchanges

2 Fruit	1/2 Fat
4 Very Lean Meat	

Calories 288
  Calories from Fat . . 54
Total Fat . . . . 6 g
  Saturated Fat . . . . . . 2 g
Cholesterol . . . . 73 mg
Sodium . . . . 255 mg
  W/o added salt . . . 166 mg
Carbohydrate . . . . . . 31 g
  Dietary Fiber . . . . . . 1 g
  Sugars . . . . 10 g
Protein . . . . 28 g

Grilled and Broiled Chicken

Most of the recipes in this section can be broiled on a charcoal grill over hot coals or placed on a heated tray under the broiler in an oven. Either method works well, but the hot coals give a special flavor to the finished dish.

Barbecue Chicken for Kids

When my children were young, this was their favorite meal. They always wanted it when their friends stayed for supper, and I happily agreed to serve it.

Serves 4 Serving Size: 1/4 recipe

- 1 (2 1/2 lb) chicken, cut in pieces, skin removed
- 1 cup catsup
- 1/4 cup sugar
- 1/4 cup cider vinegar
- 1/3 cup Worcestershire sauce
- Dash hot pepper sauce
- Nonfat cooking spray

1. Place chicken in bowl. Mix remaining ingredients together and pour over chicken. Marinate in refrigerator for 1 hour. Heat charcoal grill. Place chicken on sprayed rack 4–6 inches above coals, turning often and brushing with marinade during last 15 minutes of cooking. Grill 30 minutes.

2. **Alternate:** Brown chicken in broiler on all sides. Place in shallow baking dish. Pour marinade over and toss to coat. Bake in a preheated 350° oven for 30 minutes.

Exchanges
1 Carbohydrate
2 Lean Meat

Calories 205
   Calories from Fat . . 45
Total Fat . . . . 5 g
   Saturated Fat . . . . . . 1 g
Cholesterol . . . . 64 mg
Sodium . . . . 564 mg
Carbohydrate . . . . . . 18 g
   Dietary Fiber . . . . . . 1 g
   Sugars . . . . 10 g
Protein . . . . 21 g

Barbecue Chicken
with Peppery Sauce

Serves 8   Serving Size: 1/8 recipe

1/3 cup cider vinegar

1 tsp Worcestershire sauce

1/2 tsp onion powder

1/2 tsp salt (optional)

1/8 tsp pepper

1/2 tsp garlic powder

1 tsp chopped canned jalapeño peppers,
or 2–3 tsp fresh

1 Tbsp tomato paste

1 Tbsp olive oil

2 (2 1/2 lb) chickens, cut in pieces, skin removed

Nonfat cooking spray

1. Mix first 9 ingredients together and beat with wire whisk until smooth.

2. Heat broiler or grill. Spray rack with cooking spray. Brush chicken with marinade. Place on broiler rack and broil, turning often, brushing with marinade each turn. Broil 30 minutes in all.

Exchanges
4 Lean Meat

Calories 205
   Calories from Fat . . 72
Total Fat . . . . .8 g
   Saturated Fat . . . . . .2 g
Cholesterol . . . . .92 mg
Sodium . . . . .224 mg
   W/o added salt . . . .90 mg
Carbohydrate . . . . . . .1 g
   Dietary Fiber . . . . . .0 g
   Sugars . . . . .0 g
Protein . . . . .30 g

Breaded Broiled Chicken

Serves 4   Serving Size: 1/4 chicken

1 Tbsp oil
1 onion, sliced
1 clove garlic, crushed
1/4 lb mushrooms, sliced
1/2 tsp salt (optional)
Freshly ground pepper
1 cup white wine
1 (3 lb) chicken, quartered, skin removed
Nonfat cooking spray
1/2 cup dry bread crumbs

1. Heat oil in deep nonstick skillet. Add onion and sauté until limp.
Add garlic and mushrooms. Sauté 5 minutes. Add salt, pepper, and wine.
Bring to boil. Place chicken on top of vegetables, cover, and simmer
15 minutes. Remove chicken, reserve vegetables.

2. Spray chicken. Roll chicken in bread crumbs. Spray again. Grill over hot
coals 6–7 minutes on each side. Spray again when turning.

3. Reheat vegetables. Scatter over chicken.

Exchanges

1 Vegetable	4 Lean Meat
1 Starch	1 Fat

Calories 340
  Calories from Fat   108
Total Fat . . . . 12 g
  Saturated Fat . . . . . . 2 g
Cholesterol . . . . 92 mg
Sodium . . . . 442 mg
  W/o added salt . . . 176 mg
Carbohydrate . . . . . . 15 g
  Dietary Fiber . . . . . . 2 g
  Sugars . . . . 3 g
Protein . . . . 33 g

Broiled Chicken
with Mustard Tomato Sauce

Serves 4   Serving Size: 1/4 recipe

    Nonfat cooking spray
1   (3 lb) chicken, cut in pieces, skin removed
1   Tbsp butter
1   onion, chopped
2   Tbsp flour
1   1/2 cups low-sodium chicken broth, boiling
2   Tbsp tomato paste
2   tsp Worcestershire sauce
1   tsp sugar
1   tsp dry mustard

1. Heat broiler or grill. Spray rack. Spray chicken pieces. Broil 30 minutes, turning often, and spraying again at each turn.

2. Heat butter in saucepan. Add onion and sauté until limp. Sprinkle with flour and cook, stirring, 2–3 minutes. Remove from heat and add boiling broth, beating vigorously with wire whisk to prevent lumping. Return to heat and cook, stirring, until smooth and thick.

3. Stir in tomato paste, Worcestershire sauce, sugar, and mustard. Serve over broiled chicken.

Exchanges
4 Lean Meat
1/2 Fat

Calories 311
    Calories from Fat   114
Total Fat . . . . 13 g
    Saturated Fat . . . . . . 4 g
Cholesterol . . . . 116 mg
Sodium . . . . 189 mg
Carbohydrate . . . . . . 10 g
    Dietary Fiber . . . . . . 1 g
    Sugars . . . . 2 g
Protein . . . . 37 g

Caribbean Broiled Chicken

Serves 4   Serving Size: 1/4 recipe

- 1 (3 lb) chicken, cut in pieces, skin removed
- 2 Tbsp honey
- 1 tsp mustard
- 1 Tbsp grated fresh ginger
- 2/3 cup unsweetened pineapple juice
- 1/3 cup lite soy sauce
- 1/4 cup lemon juice
- 1 Tbsp cornstarch
- 1/4 cup dry sherry

1. Put chicken in a 9 × 9-inch baking pan. Place honey, mustard, ginger, pineapple juice, soy sauce, and lemon juice in a bowl. Beat with whisk until smooth. Pour over chicken. Cover with plastic wrap and refrigerate at least 4 hours. Turn occasionally. Remove chicken from marinade. Reserve marinade.

2. Grill chicken over hot coals, turning often and brushing with marinade, for 30 minutes.

3. Place remaining marinade in small saucepan. Bring to boil. Mix cornstarch with sherry and stir into marinade. When thickened and clear, pour over cooked chicken or serve on the side.

Exchanges
1 Fruit
4 Lean Meat

Calories 352
  Calories from Fat . . 86
Total Fat . . . . 10 g
  Saturated Fat . . . . . . 2 g
Cholesterol . . . . 108 mg
Sodium . . . . 826 mg
  with 2 Tbsp
    soy sauce . . . . . . 399 mg
Carbohydrate . . . . . . 25 g
  Dietary Fiber . . . . . . 0 g
  Sugars . . . . 10 g
Protein . . . . 37 g

Broiled Chicken with Pineapple and Currant Garnish

Serves 8   Serving Size: 1 chicken quarter

- 2 (2–2 1/2 lb) chickens, quartered, skin removed
- 1 16-oz can unsweetened pineapple slices
- 2 Tbsp oil
- 2 Tbsp lite soy sauce
- 1 tsp salt (optional)
- Freshly ground pepper
- Nonfat cooking spray
- 1 Tbsp currant jelly

1. Place chicken in a 9 × 9-inch dish. Drain pineapple, reserving juice. Add oil, soy sauce, salt, and pepper to juice. Pour over chicken. Marinate in refrigerator 1 hour, turning often. Heat broiler or grill. Spray rack with cooking spray. Drain chicken and place on rack. Broil 15 minutes, turn, and brush with marinade. Broil another 15 minutes.

2. Meanwhile, drain 8 pineapple slices and pat dry on paper towel. Heat nonstick skillet, spray, and sauté pineapple until browned on each side. Place one slice on top of each chicken quarter. Fill hole with dollop of currant jelly. Serve at once.

Exchanges
1 Fruit
4 Lean Meat

Calories 269
Calories from Fat . . 99
Total Fat . . . . 11 g
Saturated Fat . . . . . . 2 g
Cholesterol . . . . 92 mg
Sodium . . . . 495 mg
W/o added salt . . . 228 mg
Carbohydrate . . . . . . 11 g
Dietary Fiber . . . . . . 0 g
Sugars . . . . 0 g
Protein . . . . 31 g

Chicken en Brochette with Ginger Sauce

Serves 4   Serving Size: 1/4 recipe

- 3 Tbsp lite soy sauce
- 1/3 cup sherry
- 2 Tbsp sugar
- 1–2 Tbsp grated fresh ginger
- Freshly ground pepper
- 4 bamboo skewers
- 2 boneless, skinless chicken breasts, halved
- 1 bunch green onions

1. Mix soy sauce, sherry, and sugar in small saucepan. Heat to dissolve sugar. Stir in ginger and pepper. Makes 1 cup marinade.

2. Soak bamboo skewers in warm water 30 minutes. Cut chicken breasts into 1 1/2-inch cubes. Slice green onions into 1 1/2-inch lengths. Thread chicken and green onions by turns on skewers. Place in baking dish and pour marinade over all. Marinate 30 minutes. Broil 15 minutes, turning often. Serve at once.

Exchanges
3 Lean Meat

Calories	215
Calories from Fat	27
Total Fat	3 g
Saturated Fat	1 g
Cholesterol	73 mg
Sodium	781 mg
Using half soy sauce	511 mg
Carbohydrate	11 g
Dietary Fiber	0 g
Sugars	8 g
Protein	29 g

Chicken Shish Kabob

Serves 4   Serving Size: 1 skewer

> 8 small onions
> 1 tsp salt (optional)
> 2 boneless, skinless chicken breasts, halved
> 8 large mushrooms
> 2 small zucchini
> 8 (1 1/2-inch) cubes eggplant, unpeeled
> 2 Tbsp olive oil
> 2 Tbsp Balsamic vinegar
> 1 tsp granulated garlic
> 1/2 tsp salt (optional)
> Freshly ground pepper

1. Peel onions, and cut a cross in the root end of each. Place in small pot and pour boiling water over all. Add 1 tsp of salt (optional). Bring to boil, cover, and simmer 15 minutes. Drain.

2. Cut each chicken breast into 8 equal cubes. Cut zucchini into 8 equal cubes. Using 4 skewers, thread chicken, onions, mushrooms, zucchini, and eggplant in equal portions. Place kabobs in baking dish.

3. Mix next 5 ingredients together and pour over kabobs. Marinate 30 minutes, turning occasionally. Grill over hot coals 12–15 minutes, turning often. Using a long-tined meat fork, push cooked food off skewers to serve.

Exchanges

2 Vegetable   1 1/2 Fat
4 Very Lean Meat

Calories 259
　Calories from Fat . . 90
Total Fat . . . . 10 g
　Saturated Fat . . . . . . 2 g
Cholesterol . . . . 73 mg
Sodium . . . . 871 mg
　W/o added salt . . . . 72 mg
Carbohydrate . . . . . . 12 g
　Dietary Fiber . . . . . . 2 g
　Sugars . . . . 4 g
Protein . . . . 30 g

Grilled Chicken with Orange Barbecue Sauce

Serves 8   Serving Size: 1/4 chicken

1 6-oz can orange juice concentrate, undiluted
1 cup chili sauce
1/4 cup lite soy sauce
1/4 cup molasses
1 Tbsp lemon juice
1 clove garlic, crushed
2 (3 lb) chickens, quartered and skinned

1. Place first 6 ingredients in a bowl. Beat with wire whisk until smooth. Add chicken quarters and toss to coat. Marinate in refrigerator 3–4 hours, turning occasionally. Remove chicken and drain.

2. Place on heated grill and grill over charcoal or broil in the oven 40 minutes. Turn and baste with marinade every 10–15 minutes.

Exchanges
1/2 Fruit
4 Lean Meat

Calories 324
  Calories from Fat . . 81
Total Fat . . . . 9 g
  Saturated Fat . . . . . . 2 g
Cholesterol . . . . 108 mg
Sodium . . . . 816 mg
  W/o soy sauce . . . . 517 mg
Carbohydrate . . . . . . 23 g
  Dietary Fiber . . . . . . 0 g
  Sugars . . . . 3 g
Protein . . . . 37 g

Simple Marinated Broiled Chicken

Serves 8   Serving Size: 1/8 recipe

- 1/2 cup olive oil
- 1 clove garlic, crushed
- 1 tsp salt (optional)
  Freshly ground pepper
- 1 tsp dry basil
- 1 Tbsp Worcestershire sauce
- 2 (2–3 lb) chickens, cut in pieces, skin removed
  Nonfat cooking spray

1. Mix first 6 ingredients in large bowl. Add chicken and toss with marinade. Cover and marinate in refrigerator 1 hour.

2. Drain chicken, reserving marinade. Heat grill or broiler. Place chicken on sprayed rack and grill or broil, turning often, 30 minutes, brushing with marinade at each turning.

Exchanges

4 Lean Meat

Calories 218
   Calories from Fat . . 81
Total Fat . . . . 9 g
   Saturated Fat . . . . . . 2 g
Cholesterol . . . . 92 mg
Sodium . . . . 362 mg
   W/o added salt . . . . 96 mg
Carbohydrate . . . . . . 1 g
   Dietary Fiber . . . . . . 0 g
   Sugars . . . . 0 g
Protein . . . . 30 g

Chicken with Herbs, Spices, and Condiments

This chapter covers chicken dishes that depend mainly on the seasonings for their character and appealing quality.

Crispy Potato Chicken with Kale

Serves 4   Serving Size: 1/4 recipe

  1 bunch kale (or 1 10-oz pkg frozen spinach)
  1 tsp salt (optional)
  2 red potatoes
  3 Tbsp Dijon mustard
  1 clove garlic, crushed
  2 boneless, skinless chicken breasts, halved
  2 tsp olive oil
     Salt (optional) and freshly ground pepper
1/2 tsp nutmeg
     Nonfat cooking spray
1/2 cup grated Parmesan cheese

1. Wash kale. Clip green leaves from coarse center stalks. Cut leaves into bite-sized pieces. Bring large pot of water to boil. Add salt and chopped kale. Boil 5–6 minutes. Drain well, pressing out water. If using frozen spinach, defrost, and press out liquid.

2. Preheat oven to 425°. Wash potatoes, do not peel. Cut into quarters. Grate and put into ice water.

3. Mix mustard with garlic. Spread each chicken half with this. Drain shredded potatoes. Mix with olive oil. Season with salt, pepper, and nutmeg. Spray baking dish. Arrange kale (or spinach) in bottom. Arrange chicken breasts on top. Arrange potatoes on top of chicken. Sprinkle with cheese. Bake 20 minutes.

Exchanges

1 Starch	4 Lean Meat
1 Vegetable	

Calories 320
  Calories from Fat . . 99
Total Fat . . . . 10 g
  Saturated Fat . . . . . 2.5 g
Cholesterol . . . . 78 mg
Sodium . . . . 1,502 mg
  W/o added salt . . . 836 mg
Carbohydrate . . . . . . 22 g
  Dietary Fiber . . . . . . 5 g
  Sugars . . . . 3 g
Protein . . . . 34 g

Deviled Chicken Legs

Serves 6   Serving Size: 1/6 recipe

6 chicken legs with thighs, skin removed
Salt (optional), pepper, and paprika
2 Tbsp Dijon mustard
Nonfat cooking spray
4 green onions, chopped
1 tomato, peeled, seeded, chopped
1/2 lb mushrooms, sliced
2 cloves garlic, crushed
1/2 tsp dry mustard
1/4 tsp thyme
1/4 tsp crushed rosemary
3/4 cup red wine
1 cup low-sodium chicken broth

1. Season chicken with salt, pepper, and paprika. Spread with mustard. Heat large nonstick skillet and spray. Add chicken legs and brown on all sides.

2. Sprinkle with green onions, tomato, mushrooms, garlic, mustard, thyme, and rosemary. Pour on wine and stock. Bring to boil, cover, and simmer 45 minutes.

3. Remove chicken and mushrooms with spoon and place on warm serving dish. Bring cooking liquids to boil and reduce, stirring, over high heat until slightly thickened. Pour over chicken and serve.

Exchanges

1 Starch	3 Lean Meat
1 Vegetable	

Calories 360
    Calories from Fat . . 63
Total Fat . . . . 7 g
    Saturated Fat . . . . . . 2 g
Cholesterol . . . . 60 mg
Sodium . . . . 387 mg
    W/o added salt . . . 254 mg
Carbohydrate . . . . . . 22 g
    Dietary Fiber . . . . . . 3 g
    Sugars . . . . 6 g
Protein . . . . 28 g

Chicken with Herbed Yogurt

Serves 6   Serving Size: 1/6 recipe

3 boneless, skinless chicken breasts, halved
1 tsp salt (optional)
Freshly ground pepper
1 cup plain yogurt
2 Tbsp chopped fresh mint
1 Tbsp chopped fresh chives
1 clove garlic, crushed
1 Tbsp grated lemon zest
1/2 tsp pepper
1 tsp salt (optional)
2 Tbsp chili sauce
1 Tbsp sugar
1 pimiento, chopped
1 head Boston lettuce, washed
2 Tbsp chopped fresh parsley

1. Place chicken breasts in 3-quart saucepan. Cover with water, add salt and pepper. Bring to boil, cover, and simmer 20 minutes. Drain and dry. Chill.

2. Mix yogurt, mint, chives, garlic, lemon zest, pepper, salt, chili sauce, sugar, and pimiento. Arrange lettuce leaves around outside of chilled platter. Arrange chicken breasts in center. Spread with yogurt dressing and sprinkle with parsley.

Exchanges
4 Very Lean Meat
1/2 Carbohydrate

Calories 188
　Calories from Fat . . 27
Total Fat . . . . 3 g
　Saturated Fat . . . . . . 1 g
Cholesterol . . . . 73 mg
Sodium . . . . 876 mg
　W/o added salt . . . 165 mg
Carbohydrate . . . . 9 g
　Dietary Fiber . . . . . . 1 g
　Sugars . . . . 5 g
Protein . . . . 30 g

Sautéed Chicken Breasts
with Lemon Sauce

Serves 6   Serving Size: 1/6 recipe

1/2	tsp salt (optional)
1/4	cup cornmeal
1/4	cup crushed cornflakes
1/4	cup dry bread crumbs
1/4	cup flour
1	tsp each thyme and pepper
1	tsp onion powder
1/2	tsp each granulated garlic and celery seed
1	tsp oregano
3	boneless, skinless chicken breasts, halved
1/2	cup egg substitute mixed with 1/4 cup water
2	Tbsp canola oil
1	Tbsp butter
2	Tbsp flour
1	cup low-sodium chicken broth, boiling
1/2	tsp salt (optional)
	Freshly ground pepper
2	Tbsp chopped fresh chives
	Juice 1 lemon

1. Mix first 9 ingredients together in dish or zippered plastic bag. Dip chicken breasts in egg substitute mixture, then in coating.

2. Heat oil in nonstick skillet. Add chicken and sauté until browned, about 10 minutes. Cover, lower heat, and simmer 15 minutes, or until breasts resist the pressure of a fingertip.

3. Meanwhile, melt butter in small saucepan. Add flour and cook, stirring, 2–3 minutes. Remove from heat and pour in boiling broth. Beat with wire whisk to prevent lumping. Return to heat and cook, stirring, until thickened. Add salt, pepper, chives, and lemon juice. Makes 1 cup sauce. Serve with chicken.

Exchanges

1 Starch	1 1/2 Fat
4 Very Lean Meat	

Calories 293
  Calories from Fat . . 90
Total Fat . . . . 10 g
  Saturated Fat . . . . . . 2 g
Cholesterol . . . . 78 mg
Sodium . . . . 532 mg
  W/o added salt . . . 176 mg
Carbohydrate . . . . . . 19 g
  Dietary Fiber . . . . . . 1 g
  Sugars . . . . 1 g
Protein . . . . 31 g

Herbed Crumbed Drumsticks

Serves 6   Serving Size: 2 drumsticks

- 2 Tbsp Worcestershire sauce
- 2 cloves garlic, crushed
- 1/4 tsp hot pepper sauce
- 1/2 tsp salt (optional)
- Freshly ground pepper
- 1/2 cup yogurt
- 12 chicken drumsticks, skin removed
- 1 cup cracker crumbs
- 1 Tbsp oregano
- 1 tsp granulated garlic
- 1 tsp dry mustard
- 1 tsp paprika
- Nonstick cooking spray

1. Mix first 6 ingredients in a bowl. Beat with whisk until smooth. Add drumsticks and toss to coat. Marinate 3–4 hours in refrigerator.

2. Mix crumbs, oregano, granulated garlic, mustard, and paprika. Roll drumsticks in mixture. Preheat oven to 375°. Spray baking dish with cooking spray and lay drumsticks in dish. Spray drumsticks. Bake 35–40 minutes.

Exchanges

1 Starch   4 Very Lean Meat
1/2 Fat

Calories	241
Calories from Fat	48
Total Fat	5 g
Saturated Fat	1 g
Cholesterol	82 mg
Sodium	325 mg
W/o added salt	148 mg
Carbohydrate	19 g
Dietary Fiber	0 g
Sugars	1 g
Protein	28 g

Oregano Chicken Loaf

Fresh oregano can be purchased in most markets today, but if you can't find it, use 1 tsp dry. If you cannot buy ground chicken, grind it in a food processor; just be sure to remove all bones, skin, and membranes before processing.

Serves 4   Serving Size: 1/4 recipe

- 1 lb ground chicken
- 1 Tbsp canola oil
- 1 onion, chopped
- 1/4 lb mushrooms, chopped
- 2 cloves garlic, crushed
- 4 oz egg substitute
- 1/2 cup fat-free milk
- 1/2 tsp salt (optional)
- Freshly ground pepper
- 1 cup soft bread crumbs
- 3 Tbsp chopped fresh oregano
- Nonfat cooking spray

1. Preheat the oven to 350°. Place chicken in bowl. Heat oil in nonstick skillet on medium-high. Add onion and sauté, tossing, until limp. Add mushrooms and cook 5 minutes. Add garlic and cook 1 minute. Cool. Add mushroom mixture to chicken.

2. Add egg substitute and milk. Mix well. Add salt, pepper, bread crumbs, and oregano. Spray loaf pan. Put chicken mixture into pan. Smooth top and bake 45–50 minutes.

Exchanges
1/2 Starch
4 Very Lean Meat

Calories 201
   Calories from Fat . . 36
Total Fat . . . . 4 g
   Saturated Fat . . . . . . 1 g
Cholesterol . . . . 69 mg
Sodium . . . . 415 mg
   W/o added salt . . . 149 mg
Carbohydrate . . . . . . 10 g
   Dietary Fiber . . . . . . 1 g
   Sugars . . . . 3 g
Protein . . . . 31 g

Green Peppercorn Chicken with Apple

Serves 4 Serving Size: 1/4 recipe

- 1/2 cup white wine
- 1/2 cup low-sodium chicken broth
- 3 Tbsp frozen apple juice concentrate
- 2 tsp green peppercorns
- 1 tsp poultry seasoning
- 1/2 tsp granulated garlic
- 1/2 tsp salt (optional)
- 1/4 tsp nutmeg
- 2 boneless, skinless chicken breasts, halved
- 1 tart red apple
- 1 Tbsp cornstarch
- 1/4 cup water
- 1/4 cup red wine

1. Combine first 8 ingredients in large skillet. Bring to boil. Add chicken breasts. Return to boil, reduce to simmer, and cook 10 minutes.

2. Meanwhile, core apple but do not peel. Slice into 1/4-inch rings. Add to chicken mixture and simmer 10 minutes. Remove chicken and keep warm.

3. Mix cornstarch with water and wine. Stir into liquids and apple. Cook until clear and thickened. Pour over chicken breasts and serve.

Exchanges
1 Fruit
4 Very Lean Meat

Calories 228
  Calories from Fat . . 27
Total Fat . . . . 3 g
  Saturated Fat . . . . . . 1 g
Cholesterol . . . . 73 mg
Sodium . . . . 352 mg
  W/o added salt . . . . 86 mg
Carbohydrate . . . . . . 14 g
  Dietary Fiber . . . . . . 1 g
  Sugars . . . . 5 g
Protein . . . . 27 g

Chicken Picatta

Serves 4   Serving Size: 1 chicken breast half

> 2 boneless, skinless chicken breasts, halved
>   Nonfat cooking spray
> 2 cups soft bread crumbs
> 1 Tbsp granulated garlic
> 1 Tbsp parsley flakes
> 1 tsp lemon-pepper marinade
> 1/2 cup grated Parmesan cheese
>   Juice 1 lemon (about 2 Tbsp)

1. Preheat oven to 350°. Spray each chicken breast half. Mix bread crumbs, garlic, parsley flakes, lemon-pepper marinade, and cheese. Roll each breast half in this mixture.

2. Lay side by side in a shallow baking dish that has been heavily sprayed. Squeeze lemon juice over breasts. Bake 15–20 minutes, or until breasts resist the pressure of a finger.

Exchanges

1 Starch	1/2 Fat
4 Very Lean Meat	

Calories 246
  Calories from Fat . . 72
Total Fat . . . . 8 g
  Saturated Fat . . . . . . 3 g
Cholesterol . . . . 96 mg
Sodium . . . . 219 mg
Carbohydrate . . . . . . 12 g
  Dietary Fiber . . . . . . 1 g
  Sugars . . . . 1 g
Protein . . . . 32 g

Chicken Ring Mold

You can fill the center of this mold with sautéed mushrooms, rice with peas, cooked noodles with cheese, or with a chilled salad filling.

Serves 8   Serving Size: 1/8 recipe

2 lb boneless, skinless chicken
1 onion, coarsely chopped
4 egg whites
1 12-oz can evaporated fat-free milk, chilled
1 tsp salt (optional)
1/2 tsp white pepper
1/2 tsp nutmeg
1/2 cup chopped fresh chives
1/4 cup chopped fresh oregano
1/4 cup chopped pimiento
Nonfat cooking spray

1. Preheat oven to 325°. Trim chicken of fat and cut into chunks. Add with onion to food processor. Grind. With machine running, add egg whites, one at a time. Add evaporated milk, salt, pepper, and nutmeg. Put into large bowl. Stir in chives, oregano, and pimiento. Spray ring mold. Add chicken mixture to mold.

2. Place mold in baking dish. Pour boiling water in baking dish halfway up the outside of mold. Bake 45 minutes, or until a knife inserted in the middle comes out clean. Remove mold from water. Place heated serving plate over mold. Quickly invert, remove mold, and serve.

Exchanges
1/2 Skim Milk
4 Very Lean Meat

Calories 202
  Calories from Fat . . 27
Total Fat . . . . 3 g
  Saturated Fat . . . . . . 1 g
Cholesterol . . . . 75 mg
Sodium . . . . 415 mg
  W/o added salt . . . 149 mg
Carbohydrate . . . . . . 8 g
  Dietary Fiber . . . . . . 0 g
  Sugars . . . . 0 g
Protein . . . . 33 g

Chicken Wing Drumsticks (Appetizer)

Serves 12   Serving Size: 2 drumsticks

- 3 lb chicken wings
- 4 oz egg substitute
- 1 1/2 cups unseasoned bread crumbs
- Nonfat cooking spray
- Salt (optional) and pepper
- 1/2 cup white wine
- 1/2 cup Dijon mustard
- 1 tsp garlic powder
- 1 tsp dill weed
- 1 tsp sugar
- 1/2 Tbsp cornstarch, mixed with 2 Tbsp water

1. Preheat oven to 400°. Cut tiny drumsticks at the joint and remove from each chicken wing. Use wing to make stock. Remove and discard skin from drumsticks. Dip in egg substitute, then roll in bread crumbs. Spray a baking sheet and lay little drumsticks on sheet. Spray and season with salt and pepper. Bake, turning once, for 30 minutes.

2. Meanwhile, place wine, mustard, garlic powder, dill weed, and sugar in small pan. Bring to boil. Stir in cornstarch and cook until thickened and clear. Pour into small bowl. Place on large round platter. Surround with chicken wing drumsticks and serve, using sauce for dipping.

Exchanges
1/2 Starch
2 Lean Meat

Calories 150
Calories from Fat . . 36
Total Fat . . . . 4 g
Saturated Fat . . . . . . 1 g
Cholesterol . . . . 41 mg
Sodium . . . . 402 mg
W/o added salt . . . 358 mg
Carbohydrate . . . . . . 11 g
Dietary Fiber . . . . . . 1 g
Sugars . . . . 1 g
Protein . . . . 16 g

Chicken Mediterranean

Serves 6   Serving Size: 1/6 recipe

1 1/2 lb boneless, skinless chicken breasts, cut in 1-inch pieces
Salt (optional) and pepper
Nonfat cooking spray
1 onion, chopped
1 clove garlic, crushed
1 portobello mushroom, sliced
1/2 lemon, thinly sliced
3/4 cup peeled, chopped tomatoes
1/4 cup sliced pitted ripe olives
1 Tbsp chopped fresh oregano
1 Tbsp chopped fresh basil
Freshly ground pepper
1/4 cup dry white wine
3/4 cup low-sodium chicken broth
1 small green bell pepper, cut in narrow strips
1 small red bell pepper, cut in narrow strips
1 tsp sugar
1 Tbsp capers
2 Tbsp chopped fresh parsley

1. Sprinkle chicken with salt and pepper. Spray nonstick skillet. Add onion and sauté until limp. Add garlic and mushrooms and cook 4–5 minutes. Add chicken and brown. Reduce heat to low.

2. Add lemon, half the tomato, olives, oregano, basil, pepper, wine, and broth. Cover and simmer 15 minutes.

3. Remove lemon slices and discard. Add remaining tomato, sugar, and bell peppers. Cover and cook 10 minutes. Add capers. Serve sprinkled with parsley.

Exchanges

1 Vegetable	1/2 Fat
4 Very Lean Meat	

Calories 235
  Calories from Fat . . 55
Total Fat . . . . 6 g
  Saturated Fat . . . . . . 1 g
Cholesterol . . . . 87 mg
Sodium . . . . 378 mg
  W/o added salt . . . 199 mg
Carbohydrate . . . . . . 9 g
  Dietary Fiber . . . . . . 2 g
  Sugars . . . . 4 g
Protein . . . . 35 g

Chicken with Pasta

Pasta dishes, in general, are nutritionally sound. Fats are low, calories are reasonable, and cholesterol well within limits. They are excellent meals-in-one served with a tossed salad and crunchy French bread. To get the best results, cook pasta according to package instructions in a large amount of boiling water until barely tender. If you want to rinse in cold running water, you'll need to dip the pasta in very hot water right before serving. And add one of the following delicious sauces.

Chicken Farfalle

Serves 4   Serving Size: 1/4 recipe

> 6 dried porcini or shiitake mushrooms
> 1 1/2 cups low-fat chicken broth
> Nonfat cooking spray
> 2 boneless, skinless chicken breasts, halved, cubed
> 2 shallots, sliced
> 1 clove garlic, crushed
> 1/4 cup Marsala wine
> 1/2 cup fat-free or low-fat sour cream
> 2 Tbsp quick-mixing flour
> 2 Tbsp grated Parmesan cheese
> 1/2 tsp salt (optional)
> 1/4 tsp pepper
> 2 Tbsp finely chopped fresh basil
> 1/2 lb farfalle pasta, cooked, drained

1. Soak mushrooms in warm water 30 minutes; remove and chop. Pour mushroom water into chicken broth and set aside. Spray nonstick skillet. Add chicken, and cook 7 minutes. Add shallots and garlic and cook, stirring, 2–3 minutes. Spray again. Add mushrooms and cook, stirring, 3 minutes.

2. Add wine and cook, uncovered, until wine has reduced to about 1 tsp. Bring mushroom-broth mixture to boil. Meanwhile, beat sour cream with flour until smooth. Remove broth from heat and beat flour mixture into it. Return to heat and cook, stirring, until thickened.

3. Beat in cheese, salt, pepper, and basil. Add to chicken. Serve over cooked farfalle.

Exchanges
4 Starch
3 Very Lean Meat

Calories 459
  Calories from Fat . . 45
Total Fat . . . . 5 g
  Saturated Fat . . . . . . 2 g
Cholesterol . . . . 75 mg
Sodium . . . . 437 mg
  W/o added salt . . . 171 mg
Carbohydrate . . . . . . 55 g
  Dietary Fiber . . . . . . 1 g
  Sugars . . . . 2 g
Protein . . . . 39 g

Dijon Chicken with Vegetables and Fettuccine

Serves 6 Serving Size: 1/6 recipe

- 1 Tbsp olive oil
- 1 (4 lb) chicken, cut in pieces, skin removed
  Salt (optional) and freshly ground pepper
- 1 onion, thinly sliced
- 1/2 cup sliced zucchini
- 1/2 cup chopped eggplant
- 1/2 cup chopped red bell pepper
- 1 clove garlic, crushed
- 1 cup low-fat sour cream
- 1/2 cup fat-free milk
- 3 Tbsp Dijon mustard
- 1 Tbsp Balsamic vinegar
- 1 tsp sugar
- 8 oz fettuccine pasta, cooked, drained
- 1/4 cup chopped fresh parsley

1. In nonstick skillet or wok, heat oil. Season chicken with salt and pepper, and brown. Cover and cook 10 minutes, turning often. Remove from skillet. Add onion and cook until limp. Add zucchini, eggplant, and red bell pepper. Cook, stirring, 3–4 minutes. Add garlic and cook 1 minute.

2. Mix sour cream, milk, mustard, vinegar, and sugar. Beat with whisk. Return chicken to skillet. Pour in sour cream mixture and cook, covered, over low heat 20–25 minutes.

3. Put fettuccine in large warm bowl. Pour chicken and sauce over all. Sprinkle with parsley and serve.

Exchanges

2 1/2 Starch	3 Lean Meat
1 Vegetable	1/2 Fat

Calories 412
  Calories from Fat . . 108
Total Fat . . . . 12 g
  Saturated Fat . . . . . . 2 g
Cholesterol . . . . 90 mg
Sodium . . . . 485 mg
  W/o added salt . . . 317 mg
Carbohydrate . . . . . . 39 g
  Dietary Fiber . . . . . . 1 g
  Sugars . . . . 4 g
Protein . . . . 33 g

Fettuccine with Vegetables, Chicken, and Mock Alfredo Sauce

Serves 6   Serving Size: 1/6 recipe

- 1/4 lb mushrooms, sliced
- 2 Tbsp olive oil
- 3 Tbsp flour
- 1 1/2 cups fat-free milk, scalded
- 2 Tbsp chopped fresh parsley
- 1 tsp basil
- 1 tsp oregano
- 1/2 tsp granulated garlic
- 1/2 tsp salt (optional)
- Freshly ground pepper
- 8 cups water
- 1/2 lb fettuccine pasta
- 1 cup carrots, cut in thin strips
- 1 cup asparagus, cut in 1-inch pieces
- 1 cup peas
- 2 cups diced cooked chicken

1. Sauté mushrooms in olive oil 5 minutes. Sprinkle with flour and cook, stirring, 2–3 minutes. Remove from heat and add scalded milk. Beat with whisk to prevent lumping. Return to heat and cook, stirring, until thickened. Add parsley, basil, oregano, garlic, salt, and pepper.

2. Bring 8 cups water to rolling boil. Add fettuccine and carrots. Cook 5 minutes. Add asparagus and peas. Cook 3 minutes. Drain well. Place fettuccine and vegetables in warm serving bowl. Add chicken and heated sauce. Toss to mix.

Exchanges

2 1/2 Starch 3 Very Lean Meat
1 Vegetable 1 Fat

Calories 378
  Calories from Fat . . 72
Total Fat . . . . 8 g
  Saturated Fat . . . . . . 1 g
Cholesterol . . . . 59 mg
Sodium . . . . 275 mg
  W/o added salt . . . . 97 mg
Carbohydrate . . . . . . 43 g
  Dietary Fiber . . . . . . 2 g
  Sugars . . . . 8 g
Protein . . . . 32 g

Swiss Chard, Chicken, and Rotini Bake

Serves 8   Serving Size: 1/8 recipe

1/2	lb rotini, cooked, drained
1	lb Swiss chard
	Water
	Nonfat cooking spray
1	onion, sliced
1/2	lb mushrooms, sliced
1	clove garlic, crushed
1	tsp marjoram
1	Tbsp chopped chives
2	Tbsp canola oil
3	Tbsp flour
3	cups low-sodium chicken broth, boiling
1	tsp salt (optional)
	Freshly ground pepper
2	cups cubed cooked chicken
3	Tbsp grated Parmesan cheese

1. Place rotini in bottom of 9 × 6 × 2-inch baking dish. Cut coarse stalks out of Swiss chard and chop leaves. Boil 2 quarts water and cook Swiss chard 7–8 minutes. Drain and press out water.

2. Spray nonstick skillet. Add onion and cook until limp, stirring. Spray again and add mushrooms. Cook 5 minutes, stirring. Add garlic, marjoram, and chives. Cook 1 minute.

3. Heat oil in saucepan. Add flour and cook 1–2 minutes, stirring. Remove from heat and add boiling broth, beating with whisk to prevent lumping. Return to heat and cook, stirring, until thickened. Add salt and pepper.

4. Preheat oven to 350°. Scatter Swiss chard over rotini. Add chicken and cooked vegetables. Pour sauce over all. Sprinkle with Parmesan. Bake 45 minutes.

Exchanges
1 1/2 Starch 2 Very Lean Meat
1 Vegetable 1 Fat

Calories 267
  Calories from Fat . . 54
Total Fat . . . . 6 g
  Saturated Fat . . . . . . 1 g
Cholesterol . . . . 36 mg
Sodium . . . . 381 mg
  W/o added salt . . . 115 mg
Carbohydrate . . . . . . 31 g
  Dietary Fiber . . . . . . 3 g
  Sugars . . . . 3 g
Protein . . . . 20 g

Chicken Lasagna

If you can't find ground chicken, ask the butcher to grind it for you, or do it in a food processor (p. 113).

Serves 10   Serving Size: 1/10 recipe

    1 onion, chopped
    2 Tbsp olive oil
    2 lb ground chicken
    1 clove garlic, crushed
    6 oz no-salt-added tomato paste
    1 28-oz can crushed tomatoes
  3/4 cup white wine
    1 tsp salt (optional)
       Freshly ground pepper
    2 Tbsp chopped fresh basil
    1 Tbsp chopped fresh oregano
  1/4 tsp each nutmeg and thyme
    1   bay leaf
  1/2 cup chopped fresh parsley
    1 lb whole-wheat lasagna noodles, cooked, drained
       Nonfat cooking spray
    1 lb reduced-fat ricotta cheese
    8 oz shredded reduced-fat Monterey Jack cheese
    2 Tbsp grated Parmesan cheese

1. Sauté onion in oil until limp. Add chicken and cook, stirring, 5 minutes. Add garlic, tomato paste, tomatoes, wine, salt, pepper, basil, oregano, nutmeg, thyme, and bay leaf. Bring to boil, cover and simmer 20 minutes. Remove cover and cook 15 minutes. Remove bay leaf and stir in parsley.

2. Preheat oven to 350°. Spray a 9 × 13 × 2-inch baking dish. Spread spoonful of sauce in bottom of dish. Layer 1/3 lasagna noodles, 1/4 sauce, 1/3 ricotta, and 1/3 Monterey Jack cheese. Repeat 2 times. End with sauce smoothed over top. Sprinkle with cheese. Bake 45 minutes.

Exchanges

1 1/2 Starch	4 Lean Meat
1 Vegetable	

Calories 384
  Calories from Fat . .117
Total Fat . . . . .13 g
  Saturated Fat . . . . . . .4 g
Cholesterol . . . . .75 mg
Sodium . . . . .582 mg
  W/o added salt . . . .368 mg
Carbohydrate . . . . . .28 g
  Dietary Fiber . . . . . . .4 g
  Sugars . . . . .3 g
Protein . . . . .39 g

Lorraine's Microwave Chicken Breasts with Penne

Serves 4   Serving Size: 1/4 recipe

- 8 oz penne pasta, cooked, drained
- Nonfat cooking spray
- 1 garlic clove, crushed
- 1/4 cup chopped fresh parsley
- 2 boneless, skinless chicken breasts, halved
- 2 Tbsp honey
- 1 tsp lite soy sauce
- 1 Tbsp Dijon mustard
- 1/2 tsp curry powder
- 2 Tbsp grated Parmesan cheese

1. Spray cooked pasta with cooking spray and toss with garlic and parsley. Keep warm.

2. Wash chicken breasts and remove any fat. Put into sprayed microwave dish. Mix honey, soy sauce, mustard, and curry powder. Spread over chicken. Microwave on high 3–4 minutes. Turn, spread with sauce again, and microwave 3 minutes. Press chicken with finger. If meat does not resist pressure, cook 1–2 minutes more.

3. Put penne in serving dish. Sprinkle with cheese. Add chicken and pour remaining sauce over all.

Exchanges
3 1/2 Starch
4 Very Lean Meat

Calories 414
 Calories from Fat . . 54
Total Fat . . . . 6 g
 Saturated Fat . . . . . . 2 g
Cholesterol . . . . 75 mg
Sodium . . . . 357 mg
Carbohydrate . . . . . . 52 g
 Dietary Fiber . . . . . . 0 g
 Sugars . . . . 11 g
Protein . . . . 36 g

Chicken Primavera

Serves 4   Serving Size: 1/4 recipe

> 1 1/2 cups cubed boneless, skinless chicken breast
> 1/4 cup flour
> 1 tsp salt (optional)
> 1/2 tsp white pepper
> 2 Tbsp olive oil
> 3 green onions, chopped
> 1/2 cup slivered winter squash, peeled
> 1/2 cup slivered carrots
> 1/2 cup slivered zucchini
> 1 tomato, peeled, seeded, chopped
> 2 Tbsp white wine
> 1/3 cup low-sodium chicken broth
> 1 Tbsp butter
> 1 Tbsp chopped fresh basil
> Salt (optional) and pepper
> 3 cups linguini, cooked, drained
> 2 Tbsp grated Parmesan cheese

1. Roll chicken in mixture of flour, salt, and pepper. Heat oil in large skillet. Cook chicken, stirring, until no longer pink. Drain chicken on paper towels.

2. Add green onions, squash, and carrots to skillet. Cook 5–6 minutes. Add zucchini and tomatoes. Cook 1–2 minutes. Add wine, scraping up bottom. Add broth and bring to boil. Add butter, basil, salt, and pepper. Add chicken to pasta. Pour vegetables and sauce on top. Sprinkle with Parmesan and serve.

Exchanges

2 Starch   4 Very Lean Meat
1 Vegetable 2 Fat

Calories 520
  Calories from Fat . .143
Total Fat . . . . .15 g
  Saturated Fat . . . . . . .4 g
Cholesterol . . . . .119 mg
Sodium . . . . .993 mg
  W/o added salt . . . .194 mg
Carbohydrate . . . . . . .42 g
  Dietary Fiber . . . . . . .3 g
  Sugars . . . . .4 g
Protein . . . . .49 g

Stuffed Pasta Shells

Serves 6   Serving Size: 4 shells with sauce

1	onion, chopped
1	Tbsp olive oil
1	clove garlic, crushed
2	Tbsp chopped fresh basil
1	tsp oregano
1	28-oz can no-salt-added crushed tomatoes
4	Tbsp no-salt-added tomato paste
1	tsp sugar
1	tsp salt (optional)
	Freshly ground pepper
1	small onion, grated
1	clove garlic, crushed
1	lb ground chicken, p. 113
1/2	tsp salt (optional)
1/4	tsp white pepper
1/2	tsp nutmeg
2	egg whites
1/2	cup evaporated fat-free milk
1/4	cup chopped fresh chives
	Nonfat cooking spray
24	jumbo pasta shells, cooked, drained
1/4	cup grated Parmesan cheese

1. Sauté onion in olive oil until limp. Add garlic and cook 1–2 minutes. Add basil and oregano. Cook, stirring, 1 minute. Add tomatoes, tomato paste, sugar, salt, and pepper. Cover and simmer 1 hour. If too thick, add water.

2. Grate onion and garlic. Add chicken, salt, pepper, and nutmeg. Puree in blender or food processor. Add egg whites. Add evaporated milk. Stir in chives.

3. Preheat oven to 350°. Spray baking dish with cooking spray. Put 1 tsp filling in each shell and place in dish. Pour sauce over all. Sprinkle with Parmesan and bake 35–40 minutes.

Exchanges

2 Starch	2 Lean Meat
2 Vegetable	1 Fat

Calories 355
  Calories from Fat . . 63
Total Fat . . . . 7 g
  Saturated Fat . . . . . . 2 g
Cholesterol . . . . 62 mg
Sodium . . . . 722 mg
  W/o added salt . . . 189 mg
Carbohydrate . . . . . . 46 g
  Dietary Fiber . . . . . . 1 g
  Sugars . . . . 8 g
Protein . . . . 34 g

Stuffed Manicotti

Serves 8   Serving Size: 1/8 recipe

- 1 onion, minced
- 2 carrots, minced
- 1 Tbsp olive oil
- 4 Tbsp tomato paste
- 1 cup ground chicken, p. 113
- 2 cloves garlic, crushed
- 1 cup red wine
- 1 cup crushed tomatoes
- 1 tsp oregano
- 2 cups ground chicken, p. 113
- 1 onion, minced
- 2 cloves garlic, crushed
- 1/2 cup ground pork
- 1 slice bread
- 4 oz egg substitute
- 4 oz light mozzarella cheese, grated
- 1/2 tsp salt (optional)
- Freshly ground pepper
- 1/2 tsp nutmeg
- 8 oz manicotti, cooked, drained
- 1 cup chicken stock
- 8 oz plain yogurt
- 3 Tbsp quick-mixing flour
- 3 Tbsp grated Parmesan cheese

1. Sauté onion and carrots in olive oil for 5 minutes. Add tomato paste, ground chicken, and garlic. Cook, stirring, 5 minutes. Add wine, tomatoes, and oregano. Simmer 30 minutes. Add water, if too thick.

2. Mix chicken, onion, garlic, and pork. Soak bread in water 3 minutes. Squeeze water out and crumble into meat mixture. Mix in egg substitute, mozzarella, salt, pepper, and nutmeg. Put mixture in pastry bag or use a spoon to stuff it into manicotti shells. Put stuffed manicotti in baking dish. Cover with tomato sauce.

3. Preheat oven to 350°. Boil chicken stock. Mix yogurt with flour and beat with whisk until smooth. Remove stock from heat and beat yogurt mixture into it. Return to low heat and cook until thickened. Stir in grated Parmesan. Pour sauce over stuffed shells and tomato sauce. Bake 20–25 minutes.

Exchanges
2 1/2 Starch
5 Lean Meat

Calories 491
   Calories from Fat . . 99
Total Fat . . . . 11 g
   Saturated Fat . . . . . . 3 g
Cholesterol . . . . 123 mg
Sodium . . . . 444 mg
   W/o added salt . . . 310 mg
Carbohydrate . . . . . . 37 g
   Dietary Fiber . . . . . . 2 g
   Sugars . . . . 6 g
Protein . . . . 54 g

Chicken Tetrazzini

Serves 8   Serving Size: 1/8 recipe

1 (4 lb) chicken, quartered
1 onion, chopped
1 sprig parsley
1 celery stalk, chopped
1 tsp salt (optional)
4 cups water
2 Tbsp butter
1 cup sliced mushrooms
4 Tbsp flour
1/2 tsp salt (optional)
1 cup evaporated fat-free milk, scalded
1/2 cup slivered ham
1/4 cup sherry
1/2 lb spaghetti, cooked, drained
  Nonfat cooking spray
3 Tbsp grated Parmesan cheese

1. Place chicken, onion, parsley, celery, salt, and water in large pot. Simmer 1 hour. Drain, reserving liquids. Skim off fat. Over high heat, reduce liquids to 1 1/2 cups. Remove meat from chicken and discard bones and skin.

2. Boil reduced broth. Melt butter in large pan. Add mushrooms and sauté 5 minutes. Sprinkle with flour and cook, stirring, 2–3 minutes. Remove from heat, beat in boiling broth.

3. Add salt, milk, and ham. Return to heat and simmer 10 minutes. Stir in chicken and sherry.

4. Mix spaghetti with chicken and sauce. Turn into sprayed casserole. Sprinkle with Parmesan. Place in preheated 375° oven and bake until browned and bubbly (40–45 minutes).

Exchanges

1 Starch	1 Fat
3 Lean Meat	

Calories 350	
Calories from Fat . . 90	
Total Fat . . . . 10 g	
Saturated Fat . . . . . . 4 g	
Cholesterol . . . . 84 mg	
Sodium . . . . 682 mg	
W/o added salt . . . 281 mg	
Carbohydrate . . . . . . 29 g	
Dietary Fiber . . . . . . 1 g	
Sugars . . . . 2 g	
Protein . . . . 32 g	

Spaghetti à la Diable

Serves 6   Serving Size: 1/6 recipe

Nonfat cooking spray

8 oz spinach spaghetti, cooked, drained

1 onion, chopped

1 Tbsp olive oil

1 clove garlic, crushed

1 28-oz can chopped tomatoes

2 Tbsp no-salt-added tomato paste

1/2 tsp salt (optional)

Freshly ground pepper

1 Tbsp sugar

Dash hot pepper sauce

1 cup sliced mushrooms

1 Tbsp butter

1 cup diced cooked chicken

1 Tbsp Dijon mustard

1 tsp oregano

1/4 cup grated Parmesan cheese

1. Spray 2-quart casserole and put spaghetti in it. Sauté onion in oil until limp. Add garlic and cook 1 minute. Add tomatoes, paste, salt, pepper, sugar, and hot pepper sauce. Heat to boiling, reduce heat, cover, and simmer 25 minutes.

2. Preheat oven to 350°. Sauté mushrooms in butter 5 minutes. Add mushrooms, chicken, Dijon mustard, and oregano to sauce. Cook, covered, 5 minutes. Pour sauce over spaghetti. Sprinkle with cheese. Bake 20 minutes or until heated through and cheese has melted.

Exchanges

1 Starch	3 Lean Meat
2 Vegetable	1/2 Fat

Calories 272
  Calories from Fat . . 72
Total Fat . . . . 8 g
  Saturated Fat . . . . . . 3 g
Cholesterol . . . . 57 mg
Sodium . . . . 691 mg
  W/o added salt . . . 513 mg
Carbohydrate . . . . . . 25 g
  Dietary Fiber . . . . . . 1 g
  Sugars . . . . 6 g
Protein . . . . 24 g

Chicken Livers

Whenever you purchase a whole chicken, you get a small bundle with the neck, gizzard, heart, and liver. You can use the neck, gizzard, and heart to make stock but not the liver. You can freeze the livers as you get them and keep adding to the cache until you have 10 or 12, or about one pound.

Chicken livers, or any liver for that matter, are very high in cholesterol. Other than that, they are highly nutritious. If you like liver, here are some ways to serve it.

Chicken Livers en Brochette

Serves 4   Serving Size: 1/4 recipe

- 6 chicken livers (1/2 lb)
- 6 slices bacon, cut in half
- 12 mushrooms
- 16 1 1/2-inch squares of red bell pepper
- Freshly ground pepper
- Nonfat cooking spray
- 4 bamboo skewers, soaked 30 min in water

1. Cut livers in half, removing membrane. Place bacon in frying pan and pour boiling water over all. Simmer 7 minutes, drain. Trim mushroom stalks, leaving mushroom whole. Wrap each chicken liver in bacon slice.

2. Thread red pepper on skewer. Add wrapped liver, mushroom, and another pepper. Repeat twice, ending with red pepper.

3. Sprinkle kabobs with pepper. Heat broiler or grill. Spray tray or grill. Spray kabobs. Grill or broil 20 minutes, turning often, or until bacon is crisp.

Exchanges
1 Lean Meat
1 Fat

Calories	120
Calories from Fat	63
Total Fat	7 g
Saturated Fat	2 g
Cholesterol	230 mg
Sodium	170 mg
Carbohydrate	2 g
Dietary Fiber	1 g
Sugars	1 g
Protein	12 g

Chicken Liver Omelet

Serves 2   Serving Size: 1/2 omelet

> 2 large chicken livers, halved, membranes removed
> Butter-flavored nonfat cooking spray
> 1 small onion, sliced
> 1 clove garlic, crushed
> 1/2 cup mushrooms, sliced
> Salt (optional) and freshly ground pepper
> 1/2 tsp rosemary
> 1 whole egg
> 4 oz egg substitute
> 1 Tbsp butter

1. Cube chicken livers. Spray nonstick skillet and add onion. Sauté, stirring, until limp. Spray again. Add garlic and mushrooms. Sauté, stirring, 5 minutes. Sprinkle with salt, pepper, and rosemary. Spray again and add livers. Sauté, stirring, until cooked. Keep warm.

2. Mix egg and egg substitute. Heat nonstick skillet and add butter. When sizzling hot, add eggs. Scramble with fork. Move batter around to cover surface of skillet. Allow omelet to set, but not dry out. Loosen with spatula.

3. Arrange liver mixture on half of omelet. Fold remaining half over. Slide omelet from skillet, turning it over. Cut in half to serve.

Exchanges

1 Vegetable   1/2 Fat
2 Lean Meat

Calories 183	
Calories from Fat . . 90	
Total Fat . . . . 10 g	
Saturated Fat . . . . . . 5 g	
Cholesterol . . . . 243 mg	
Sodium . . . . 316 mg	
W/o added salt . . . 188 mg	
Carbohydrate . . . . . . 10 g	
Dietary Fiber . . . . . . 2 g	
Sugars . . . . 2 g	
Protein . . . . 14 g	

Chinese Chicken Livers

Serves 4   Serving Size: 1/4 recipe

1 lb chicken livers

4 cups boiling water

2 green onions

2 cups low-sodium chicken broth

1 Tbsp oyster sauce

1 Tbsp lite soy sauce

1 Tbsp sherry

1 tsp sugar

2 tsp cornstarch

2 Tbsp water

2 Tbsp finely chopped cooked ham

1. Put chicken livers in bowl. Pour on boiling water. Stir well, then drain. Rinse in cold water and drain. Cut in quarters, removing membrane.

2. Mince green onions. Put in saucepan with broth, oyster sauce, soy sauce, sherry, and sugar. Bring to boil. Add livers, reduce heat, and simmer, covered, 3–4 minutes.

3. Blend cornstarch with water. Stir into livers, and cook until clear and thick. Turn onto serving dish and sprinkle with ham.

Exchanges
1/2 Carbohydrate
2 Lean Meat

Calories 142
  Calories from Fat . . 36
Total Fat . . . . 4 g
  Saturated Fat . . . . . . 1 g
Cholesterol . . . . 447 mg
Sodium . . . . 393 mg
  With 1/2 soy sauce
  and 1/2 oyster
  sauce . . . . 229 mg
Carbohydrate . . . . 5 g
  Dietary Fiber . . . . . . 0 g
  Sugars . . . . 1 g
Protein . . . . 19 g

Curried Chicken Livers

Serves 4   Serving Size: 1/4 recipe

  1 lb chicken livers
  1 Tbsp canola oil
    Salt (optional) and freshly ground pepper
  2 green onions, chopped
  1 clove garlic, crushed
  1 Tbsp curry powder
  1 Tbsp flour
  1 cup low-sodium chicken broth, boiling
  2 Tbsp red wine
1/2 cup raisins
  2 Tbsp chopped almonds

1. Remove membrane and cut livers in half. Heat oil in skillet. Add livers and sauté quickly, seasoning with salt and pepper. Remove from skillet.

2. Add onion to skillet. Sauté until limp. Add garlic and sauté 1–2 minutes, stirring. Sprinkle with curry powder and flour. Sauté 2–3 minutes, stirring. Remove from heat and pour on boiling broth. Beat with whisk to prevent lumping. Return to heat and cook, stirring, until thickened.

3. Add wine and chicken livers. Cook 2–3 minutes. Add raisins and almonds. Serve over rice.

Exchanges
1 1/2 Carbohydrate   1 Fat
2 Lean Meat

Calories 290
  Calories from Fat   117
Total Fat . . . . 13 g
  Saturated Fat . . . . . . 3 g
Cholesterol . . . . 448 mg
Sodium . . . . 294 mg
  W/o added salt . . . 161 mg
Carbohydrate . . . . . . 21 g
  Dietary Fiber . . . . . . 2 g
  Sugars . . . . 12 g
Protein . . . . 22 g

Marsala Chicken Livers en Linguini

Serves 4   Serving Size: 1/4 recipe

> 1/2 lb chicken livers
>
> 2 Tbsp butter
>
> 1/2 lb mushrooms, sliced
>
> 1 cup asparagus pieces
>
> 1/4 tsp each thyme and oregano
>
> 2 Tbsp flour
>
> 1 cup low-sodium chicken broth, boiling
>
> 2 Tbsp Marsala wine
>
> 3 Tbsp nonfat sour cream
>
> Salt (optional) and freshly ground pepper
>
> 8 oz linguini, cooked and drained

1. Remove membrane and cut livers in small pieces.

2. Melt butter in large nonstick skillet. Add livers, mushrooms, asparagus, thyme, and oregano. Cook until livers are browned and vegetables tender. Sprinkle with flour and cook 2–3 minutes, stirring. Remove from heat and pour on boiling broth, beating with whisk to prevent lumping. Stir in wine and sour cream. Season to taste. Serve over hot linguini.

Exchanges

3 Starch	1 Lean Meat
1 Vegetable	1 1/2 Fat

Calories 397
  Calories from Fat . . 108
Total Fat . . . . 12 g
  Saturated Fat . . . . . . 6 g
Cholesterol . . . . 237 mg
Sodium . . . . 360 mg
  W/o added salt . . . 296 mg
Carbohydrate . . . . . . 50 g
  Dietary Fiber . . . . . . 1 g
  Sugars . . . . 4 g
Protein . . . . 20 g

Rumaki (Appetizer)

Serves 6   Serving Size: 3 pieces

6 chicken livers

6 slices bacon

3 Tbsp Dijon mustard

Freshly ground pepper

Nonfat cooking spray

1. Remove membrane and cut livers into 18 small pieces.

2. Cut each bacon slice into 3 pieces. Place bacon in skillet. Pour on boiling water and simmer 8 minutes. Remove and drain.

3. Spread liver pieces with dab of mustard. Sprinkle with pepper. Wrap each in piece of bacon and skewer with toothpick. Spray baking sheet with cooking spray. Put liver bundles on sheet. Put in preheated 375° oven and bake 15 minutes.

Exchanges

1 Medium-Fat Meat

Calories 83
   Calories from Fat . . 45
Total Fat . . . . 5 g
   Saturated Fat . . . 1 1/2 g
Cholesterol . . . . 153 mg
Sodium . . . . 291 mg
   With half Dijon . . . 202 mg
Carbohydrate . . . . 1 g
   Dietary Fiber . . . . . . 0 g
   Sugars . . . . 0 g
Protein . . . . 8 g

Sweet and Sour Chicken Livers

Serves 4   Serving Size: 1/4 recipe

> 1 cup rice
> 1/2 onion, finely chopped
> 1/4 cup finely chopped green pepper
> 3 Tbsp brown sugar
> 1/2 tsp salt (optional)
> Freshly ground pepper
> 1/4 cup vinegar
> 1 lb chicken livers
> Nonfat cooking spray
> 1/4 cup water
> 1/4 cup bacon bits

1. Cook rice. Place onion, green pepper, sugar, salt, pepper, and vinegar in bowl. Remove membrane and cut liver pieces in half.

2. Spray nonstick skillet. Add livers and sauté over medium heat 3–4 minutes. Add vinegar mixture, cover, and cook 10 minutes. Add water and cook 5 minutes.

3. Serve livers on rice with sprinkling of bacon bits.

Exchanges

1 1/2 Starch   3 Lean Meat
1 Vegetable

Calories 322
   Calories from Fat . . 72
Total Fat . . . . 8 g
   Saturated Fat . . . . . . 2 g
Cholesterol . . . . 715 mg
Sodium . . . . 497 mg
   W/o added salt . . . 296 mg
Carbohydrate . . . . . . 30 g
   Dietary Fiber . . . . . . 1 g
   Sugars . . . . 1 g
Protein . . . . 31 g

Chicken with Rice or Grains

Chicken and rice naturally go together. One compliments the other. Any number of herb, condiment, spice, and vegetable combinations can be combined with these two staples. This holds true for most grains. Most of the following recipes are meals-in-one and can be served with crusty bread and a salad.

Apricot East Indian Chicken with Rice

Serves 4 Serving Size: 1/4 recipe

2 1/2 cups low-sodium chicken broth

2 cloves garlic, crushed

1/2 tsp cinnamon

1 tsp ground coriander

1 tsp cumin

1 tsp onion powder

1 Tbsp grated fresh ginger

1/2 tsp turmeric

1/2 tsp salt (optional)

Dash cayenne pepper

1/2 cup chopped dried apricots

1 cup uncooked long-grain rice

2 boneless, skinless chicken breasts, cubed

1 cup peas

1. Put broth, garlic, cinnamon, coriander, cumin, onion powder, ginger, turmeric, salt, cayenne, and apricots in Dutch oven. Bring to boil. Stir in rice, return to boil, cover, lower heat, and simmer 10 minutes.

2. Add chicken, cover, and simmer 10 minutes. Add peas, cover, and cook 5 minutes. Keep heat low and stir occasionally for 15 minutes or until rice and chicken are done. Fluff with fork and serve.

Exchanges

3 Starch	3 Very Lean
1 Fruit	Meat

Calories 404
Calories from Fat . . 36
Total Fat . . . . 4 g
Saturated Fat . . . . . . 1 g
Cholesterol . . . . 73 mg
Sodium . . . . 378 mg
W/o added salt . . . 111 mg
Carbohydrate . . . . . . 56 g
Dietary Fiber . . . . . . 3 g
Sugars . . . . 9 g
Protein . . . . 34 g

Apricot-Glazed
Rock Cornish Game Hens

Serves 6   Serving Size: 1/2 bird

   3 (2 lb) Cornish hens
1 1/2 cups cooked wild rice
       Nonfat cooking spray
   1 onion, grated
   1 carrot, grated
   2 stalks celery, finely chopped
   1 tsp salt (optional)
       Freshly ground pepper
   6 dried apricots, soaked in water 30 minutes, chopped
 1/2 cup apricot jam
   2 Tbsp sherry

1. Wash hens. Put wild rice in bowl. Spray nonstick skillet and heat. Add onion, carrot, and celery. Cook, stirring, until onion is translucent. Spray when necessary. Add to wild rice. Mix in salt, pepper, and apricots. Stuff hens with mixture. Close with toothpicks and tie legs together. Force wing tips back and under bird to form a stand.

2. Spray baking dish and put in hens. Spray birds. Place in preheated 350° oven and bake 30 minutes. Melt jam with sherry in pan. Brush hens with mixture. Bake 10 minutes. Brush with glaze and bake 10 minutes. Repeat once more.

3. Remove toothpicks and untie legs. Cut birds in half down the center with shears. Arrange the stuffing in six mounds on heated platter. Place bird halves on the rice.

Exchanges

2 Starch   4 Lean Meat
1 Vegetable

Calories 343
   Calories from Fat . . 36
Total Fat . . . . 4 g
   Saturated Fat . . . . . . 1 g
Cholesterol . . . . 97 mg
Sodium . . . . 460 mg
   W/o added salt . . . 106 mg
Carbohydrate . . . . . . 35 g
   Dietary Fiber . . . . . . 2 g
   Sugars . . . . 20 g
Protein . . . . 38 g

Braised Chicken with Couscous

Serves 6   Serving Size: 1/6 recipe

2	cloves garlic, crushed
1	tsp basil
1	tsp salt (optional)
1	(3 lb) chicken, cut in pieces, skin removed
1	Tbsp canola oil
1	small onion, chopped
1/2	green pepper, chopped
4	large tomatoes, peeled, seeded, chopped
2	oz ham, diced
1/2	cup low-sodium chicken broth
	Freshly ground pepper
1	10 1/2-oz pkg frozen peas
1	Tbsp capers
1	canned pimiento, chopped
1 1/2	cups quick-cooking couscous
1/4	cup grated Parmesan cheese

1. Mix garlic, basil, and salt. Rub mixture into chicken. Heat oil in casserole. Brown chicken on all sides. Remove.

2. Add onions and green pepper to casserole. Sauté, stirring, until onion is limp. Add tomatoes, ham, and chicken broth. Bring to boil, cover, and cook 10 minutes. Return chicken to casserole. Cover and simmer 30 minutes. Remove chicken and keep warm.

3. Add pepper, peas, capers, and pimiento. Stir in couscous. Simmer 10 minutes or until all liquid is gone. Arrange couscous and vegetables on heated platter. Top with chicken. Sprinkle with Parmesan and serve.

Exchanges

3 Starch	3 Lean Meat
1 Vegetable	1/2 Fat

Calories 470
  Calories from Fat . . 97
Total Fat . . . . 11 g
  Saturated Fat . . . . . . 3 g
Cholesterol . . . . 81 mg
Sodium . . . . 750 mg
  W/o added salt and
  1/2 the ham . . . . . 387 mg
Carbohydrate . . . . . . 52 g
  Dietary Fiber . . . . . 11 g
  Sugars . . . . 8 g
Protein . . . . 39 g

Barley and Chicken Pilaf

Serves 4   Serving Size: 1/4 recipe

Nonfat cooking spray

1 onion, chopped

1 boneless, skinless chicken breast, cubed

2 cloves garlic, crushed

Salt (optional) and freshly ground pepper

1 tsp basil

1/2 tsp tarragon

1/2 tsp celery seed

1 cup pearl barley

3 cups low-sodium chicken broth

1 bay leaf

2 cups broccoli florets or asparagus pieces

1/2 cup chopped fresh parsley

1. Preheat oven to 350°. Spray Dutch oven. Add onion and sauté until onion is limp. Add chicken breast and cook, stirring, until chicken is no longer pink. Spray as needed.

2. Add garlic, salt, pepper, basil, tarragon, and celery seed. Cook 1 minute. Add barley, spray, and cook, stirring, 2 minutes. Add boiling broth and bay leaf. Bring to boil, cover, and place in oven. Bake 30 minutes.

3. Add vegetable, cover, and bake 15 minutes, or until all liquid has been absorbed. Remove and discard bay leaf. Stir in parsley.

Exchanges

3 Starch	1 Very Lean
1 Vegetable	Meat

Calories 301
  Calories from Fat . . 27
Total Fat . . . . 3 g
  Saturated Fat . . . . . . 1 g
Cholesterol . . . . 37 mg
Sodium . . . . 236 mg
  W/o added salt . . . 103 mg
Carbohydrate . . . . . . 47 g
  Dietary Fiber . . . . . 10 g
  Sugars . . . . 2 g
Protein . . . . 22 g

Brown Rice, Chicken, and Vegetable Casserole

Serves 4   Serving Size: 1/4 recipe

Nonfat cooking spray
2 boneless, skinless chicken breasts, halved
1/2 tsp paprika
1 cup brown rice
2 1/4 cups low-sodium chicken broth, boiling
1 tsp salt (optional)
1 cup broccoli florets
1 cup corn niblets
1/2 cup chopped red bell pepper
1 cup peas
Freshly ground pepper
1/2 tsp marjoram
1/2 tsp dry mustard
3 Tbsp grated Parmesan cheese

1. Preheat oven to 350°. Spray casserole or Dutch oven. Heat to sizzling and add chicken. Brown on each side, spraying as needed. Remove chicken and sprinkle with paprika.

2. Add rice to casserole. Spray. Sauté, tossing, 1 minute. Remove from heat and pour on chicken broth. Return to heat and bring to boil. Add salt. Cover, place in oven, and bake 20 minutes.

3. Add broccoli, corn, bell pepper, and peas. Add pepper, marjoram, and mustard. Arrange chicken on top. Sprinkle with grated Parmesan, cover, return to oven, and bake 30–35 minutes, or until all liquid has been absorbed.

Exchanges
3 Starch
4 Very Lean Meat

Calories 410
   Calories from Fat . . 54
Total Fat . . . . 6 g
   Saturated Fat . . . . . . 2 g
Cholesterol . . . . 77 mg
Sodium . . . . 764 mg
   W/o added salt . . . 236 mg
Carbohydrate . . . . . . 49 g
   Dietary Fiber . . . . . . 6 g
   Sugars . . . . 4 g
Protein . . . . 37 g

Chicken with Garlic, Mustard, and Rice

Serves 4   Serving Size: 1/4 recipe

    1 cup low-fat sour cream
1/2 tsp salt (optional)
      Freshly ground pepper
    3 Tbsp Dijon mustard
2/3 cup fat-free milk
    2 cloves garlic, crushed
      Nonfat cooking spray
    2 boneless, skinless chicken breasts, halved
1/2 tsp tarragon
1/2 tsp rosemary
    1 Tbsp butter
    1 cup asparagus pieces
    1 green or red bell pepper, cut in strips
    2 cups hot cooked rice
1/2 tsp paprika

1. Set oven to broil. Mix first 6 ingredients. Set aside. Spray broiler pan. Lay chicken side by side on pan. Spray chicken. Sprinkle with tarragon and rosemary. Broil 15 minutes, turning once and spraying.

2. Melt butter in skillet. Add asparagus and bell pepper. Cook, covered, until crisp-tender. Stir in sour cream mixture and rice. Heat, stirring. Put in heated serving dish.

3. Arrange chicken over rice and sprinkle with paprika.

Exchanges

2 Starch   4 Very Lean Meat
1 Vegetable 1 1/2 Fat

Calories 397
   Calories from Fat . . 99
Total Fat . . . . 11 g
   Saturated Fat . . . . . . 3 g
Cholesterol . . . . 100 mg
Sodium . . . . 738 mg
   W/o added salt . . . 472 mg
Carbohydrate . . . . . . 34 g
   Dietary Fiber . . . . . . 2 g
   Sugars . . . . 2 g
Protein . . . . 34 g

Chicken and Rice à la Provence

Serves 8   Serving Size: 1/8 recipe

	Nonfat cooking spray
1/2	lb Italian sausage, thinly sliced
8	boneless, skinless chicken thighs, halved
	Salt (optional) and freshly ground pepper
1	onion, chopped
2	cups sliced mushrooms
2	cloves garlic, crushed
1	tsp each basil, oregano, and marjoram
1/4	tsp hot pepper flakes
1	cup rice
1	28-oz can no-salt-added tomatoes
1/2	cup dry white wine
1 1/2	cups low-sodium chicken broth
1	zucchini, thinly sliced
1/4	cup grated Parmesan cheese

1. Spray nonstick skillet and heat. Add sausage and brown. Remove and drain on paper towels. Brown chicken. Drain on paper towels. Sprinkle with salt and pepper.

2. Discard all drippings in skillet, except 1 Tbsp. Sauté onion until limp. Add mushrooms, garlic, basil, oregano, marjoram, and pepper flakes. Cook 4–5 minutes, stirring. Add rice and cook 1 minute. Add tomatoes, wine, broth, and bring to boil.

3. Add sausage and chicken. Return to boil. Cover and simmer 30 minutes, stirring occasionally. Add zucchini. Cook 5 minutes. Add water if necessary. Sprinkle with Parmesan before serving. (If you omit sausage, calories from fat are 116.)

Exchanges

1 Starch	1 Vegetable
4 Medium-Fat Meat	1 Fat

Calories 467
  Calories from Fat . . 192
Total Fat . . . . 21 g
  Saturated Fat . . . . . . 5 g
Cholesterol . . . . 126 mg
Sodium . . . . 433 mg
  W/o sausage . . . . . .172 mg
Carbohydrate . . . . . . 28 g
  Dietary Fiber . . . . . . 2 g
  Sugars . . . . 4 g
Protein . . . . 37 g

Curried Chicken
with Apples and Currants

Serves 6   Serving Size: 1/6 recipe

  2 Tbsp canola oil
  2 boneless, skinless chicken breasts, cubed
    Salt (optional) and pepper
  1 onion, chopped
1/2 cup finely chopped red bell pepper
1/2 cup finely chopped green bell pepper
1–2 Tbsp curry powder (to taste)
1/2 tsp garlic powder
  3 Tbsp flour
  2 cups low-sodium chicken broth, boiling
1/2 cup evaporated fat-free milk, scalded
    Juice 1/2 lemon
  1 apple cored, peeled, finely chopped
1/2 cup currants
  3 cups water
1 1/2 cups long-grain rice
    Commercial chutney (optional)
    Chopped almonds (optional)

1. Heat oil in large skillet. Add chicken, salt, and pepper. Sauté until browned. Remove. Add onion, red pepper, and green pepper. Sauté until onion is limp. Sprinkle with curry powder, garlic powder, and flour. Cook, stirring constantly, 2–3 minutes.

2. Off heat, add boiling broth. Beat with whisk to prevent lumping. Return to heat and cook, stirring often, until thickened. Add evaporated milk and lemon juice. Add apple, currants, and chicken. Cook, stirring until chicken is done (10 minutes).

3. Meanwhile, bring 3 cups water to the boil. Add rice, cover, and simmer 20 minutes or until liquid is gone. Serve chicken over rice. Pass almonds and chutney around.

Exchanges

3 Starch	2 Very Lean Meat
1 Fruit	1 Fat

Calories 410	
Calories from Fat . . 72	
Total Fat . . . . 8 g	
Saturated Fat . . . . . . 1 g	
Cholesterol . . . . 49 mg	
Sodium . . . . 183 mg	
W/o added salt . . . . 93 mg	
Carbohydrate . . . . . . 60 g	
Dietary Fiber . . . . . . 3 g	
Sugars . . . . 4 g	
Protein . . . . 25 g	

Quinoa (or Rice) Stuffed Green Peppers

Serves 4   Serving Size: 1 pepper

4	large green bell peppers
2	cups water
1	tsp salt (optional)
1	cup rinsed quinoa or rice
1	Tbsp olive oil
1	bunch green onions
8	mushrooms, chopped
1/4	cup grated Parmesan cheese
	Freshly ground pepper
1	tsp rosemary, crumbled
2	cups ground cooked chicken
1/4	cup egg substitute
3	large tomatoes, peeled, seeded, chopped
1/2	cup low-sodium chicken broth
1	tsp paprika
1	tsp Worcestershire sauce
1/2	tsp sugar
2	Tbsp cornstarch
2	Tbsp cold water
2	Tbsp chopped fresh parsley

1. Cut stem ends off peppers and save them. Remove seeds and inner white ribs. Boil 2 cups water. Add salt, and stir in quinoa (or rice). Turn heat to simmer, cover, and cook 15–20 minutes or until liquid is absorbed. Cool.

2. Heat oil in nonstick skillet. Add green onions and chopped mushrooms. Sauté 5 minutes. Add to quinoa.

3. Mix in cheese, pepper, rosemary, and ground chicken. Stir in egg substitute. Stuff peppers with mixture. Top with stem-end caps.

4. Preheat oven to 350°. Place tomato and broth in bottom of large pot. Sprinkle with paprika. Add peppers with caps on, standing upright. Bring to boil, cover with foil, and place in oven. Bake 45 minutes. Remove foil and bake 15 minutes. Remove peppers and keep warm.

5. Whisk pan liquids. Add Worcestershire sauce and sugar. Dissolve cornstarch in 2 Tbsp cold water. Stir into tomato sauce. Cook until clear and thickened. Stir in parsley. Pour over peppers and serve.

Exchanges

2 1/2 Starch   4 Lean Meat
1 Vegetable

Calories 439
   Calories from Fat . . 99
Total Fat . . . . 11 g
   Saturated Fat . . . . . . 3 g
Cholesterol . . . . 78 mg
Sodium . . . . 784 mg
   W/o added salt . . . 251 mg
Carbohydrate . . . . . . 45 g
   Dietary Fiber . . . . . . 4 g
   Sugars . . . . 5 g
Protein . . . . 39 g

Anise-Flavored Sauce
with Chicken over Couscous

Serves 6   Serving Size: 1/6 recipe

 3 cups cooked warm couscous
   Nonfat cooking spray
 2 boneless, skinless chicken breasts, in thin strips
   Salt (optional) and freshly ground pepper
 3 green onions, chopped
 1 cup chopped mushrooms
 1 cup chopped fennel (bottom portion only)
 1 cup asparagus pieces
 2 cloves garlic, crushed
 2 Tbsp chopped fresh basil
 1 lb ripe tomatoes, peeled, seeded, chopped
3/4 cup low-sodium chicken broth
   Freshly ground pepper
 2 Tbsp honey
 2 Tbsp lite soy sauce
 1 Tbsp cornstarch
1/4 cup red wine

1. Spray wok or frying pan. Add chicken. Season with salt and pepper and sauté until no longer pink. Remove from wok.

2. Spray wok again. Add green onions, mushrooms, fennel, asparagus, garlic, and basil. Sauté, stirring, 2–3 minutes. Add tomatoes. Cook 5 minutes. Add chicken broth, pepper, honey, and soy sauce. Cook 8–10 minutes.

3. Return chicken to wok. Dissolve cornstarch in wine and stir into wok. Cook until clear and thickened. Serve over warm couscous.

Exchanges

2 Starch	2 Very Lean
1 Vegetable	Meat

Calories 267
  Calories from Fat . . 27
Total Fat . . . . 3 g
  Saturated Fat . . . . . . 1 g
Cholesterol . . . . 49 mg
Sodium . . . . 371 mg
  W/o added salt . . . 282 mg
Carbohydrate . . . . . . 34 g
  Dietary Fiber . . . . . . 5 g
  Sugars . . . . 8 g
Protein . . . . 24 g

Chicken, Rice, and Beans

Serves 8   Serving Size: 1/8 recipe

    2 lb chicken legs, skin removed
  1/2 tsp salt (optional)
      Freshly ground pepper
    1 Tbsp canola oil
    1 onion, chopped
    1 green bell pepper, seeded, chopped
    1 cup rice
    1 8-oz can tomato paste
    2 cups water
  1/2 cup sliced black olives
    1 Tbsp chopped canned jalapeños
    1 14-oz can low-sodium garbanzo beans, drained
    1 14-oz can low-sodium kidney beans, drained
    2 Tbsp chopped fresh parsley

1. Preheat oven to 350°. Season chicken with salt and pepper. Brown under broiler. In 3-quart oven casserole, heat oil. Add onion and bell pepper, and sauté until onion is limp.

2. Add rice and cook, stirring, 1–2 minutes. Add tomato paste, water, olives, jalapeños, garbanzo beans, and kidney beans. Add chicken legs. Bring to boil, cover, place in oven, and bake 25–30 minutes or until liquid is gone and rice is fluffy. Sprinkle with parsley and serve.

Exchanges

2 1/2 Starch   4 Lean Meat
1 Vegetable

Calories 448
  Calories from Fat   135
Total Fat . . . . 15 g
  Saturated Fat . . . . . . 3 g
Cholesterol . . . . 101 mg
Sodium . . . . 537 mg
  W/o added salt . . . 404 mg
Carbohydrate . . . . . . 40 g
  Dietary Fiber . . . . . . 6 g
  Sugars . . . . 1 g
Protein . . . . 38 g

Curried Rice, Shrimp, and Chicken

Serves 6   Serving Size: 1/6 recipe

1 (2 1/2) lb chicken, skinned, boned, cut in pieces
Salt (optional)
Freshly ground pepper
Nonfat cooking spray
2 Tbsp butter
1 onion, chopped
1/2 green bell pepper, chopped
1/2 red bell pepper, chopped
2 cloves garlic, crushed
1 Tbsp curry powder
1 cup long-grain rice
1/2 cup dry white wine
2 cups low-sodium chicken broth
1 bay leaf
1/2 lb shelled, deveined fresh shrimp
1/2 cup commercial chutney

1. Set oven to broil. Season chicken with salt and pepper. Spray with cooking spray. Place under broiler and brown on both sides.

2. Melt butter in casserole. Add onion and peppers, and sauté until onion is limp. Add garlic and cook 1–2 minutes, stirring. Sprinkle with curry powder and cook 1 minute. Add rice and cook, stirring, 2–3 minutes. Add wine, chicken broth, and bay leaf. Bring to boil. Add chicken, reduce heat, cover and simmer 15 minutes, or until most of liquid is gone. Add shrimp, cover, and simmer 5 minutes, or until all liquid is absorbed. Serve chutney on the side.

Exchanges

1 1/2 Starch	1 Vegetable
1 Fruit	4 Lean Meat

Calories 408
  Calories from Fat . . 93
Total Fat . . . . 10 g
  Saturated Fat . . . . . . 4 g
Cholesterol . . . . 129 mg
Sodium . . . . 362 mg
  W/o added salt . . . 184 mg
Carbohydrate . . . . . . 42 g
  Dietary Fiber . . . . . . 3 g
  Sugars . . . . 14 g
Protein . . . . 30 g

Roasted Chicken

Roasting is baking the chicken in dry heat, uncovered, for varying lengths of time. This is probably the oldest and most popular way to prepare chicken. But be forewarned, roasting increases the fat content of the chicken more than most other methods of preparation. Check the nutrition facts column and adjust the serving size if the fat content is too high for you. You can roast the chicken in its skin to make it juicier; and remove the skin after the chicken is cooked.

A wonderful method of cooking a large stuffed bird is to use an outdoor grill that has a cover and is large enough to enclose the whole bird. You place mounded coals on either side of a $9 \times 6 \times 2$-inch baking dish that is used as a drip pan. Light the coals. When coals are ready, place the cooking grate over both drip pan and hot charcoal. Place dressed chicken over the drip pan, cover and roast, leaving cover vents open. An 8-pound capon should take no longer than 1 1/4 hours (in a 350° oven, it's 3 hours). The result is spectacular. A 20-pound stuffed turkey takes 3–3 1/2 hours with this method. Watch the capon and wiggle the leg after 1 hour to see if it is done. It will wiggle freely when fully cooked. Use drippings in the drip pan for the gravy.

Casserole Roasted Chicken

Serves 6   Serving Size: 1/3 of one half

> 1 (4 lb) roasting chicken
> 1 tsp salt (optional)
>   Freshly ground pepper
> 1/2 cup flour
>   Nonfat cooking spray
> 1 small onion, chopped
> 1 clove garlic, crushed
> 1/2 cup diced carrots
> 1/2 cup diced celery
> 1 cup low-sodium chicken broth
> 1 cup sliced mushrooms
> 1 Tbsp butter

1. Preheat oven to 325°. Remove skin from chicken. Using sharp knife or shears, cut chicken in half down middle. Remove backbone and keep for making stock. Salt and pepper halves. Roll in flour. Heat nonstick skillet and spray with cooking spray. Brown chicken on each side over high heat, spraying as needed. Remove from pan.

2. Spray skillet again. Add onion, garlic, carrots, and celery. Cook, stirring, until onion is limp.

3. Place chicken halves in baking dish, flesh side up. Scatter vegetables on top. Pour broth into dish. Cover tightly with aluminum foil. Roast in oven 1 hour.

4. Meanwhile, sauté mushrooms in 1 Tbsp butter for 5 minutes. Scatter mushrooms over chicken. Raise temperature to 350° and roast uncovered for 15 minutes.

Exchanges

1/2 Starch	4 Lean Meat
1 Vegetable	

Calories	285
Calories from Fat	94
Total Fat	10 g
Saturated Fat	3 g
Cholesterol	101 mg
Sodium	490 mg
W/o added salt	134 mg
Carbohydrate	13 g
Dietary Fiber	1 g
Sugars	2 g
Protein	33 g

Chinese Roast Stuffed Chicken

Serves 8   Serving Size: 1/8 recipe

> 1 (4 1/2 lb) roasting chicken
> Salt (optional) and pepper
> 1 Tbsp canola oil
> 1/2 lb mushrooms, sliced
> 3 slices fresh ginger, chopped
> 1 bunch green onions, chopped
> 1 Tbsp sugar
> 2 Tbsp lite soy sauce
> 1/4 cup sherry
> 1 cup low-sodium chicken broth
> 1 Tbsp cornstarch
> 2 Tbsp sherry

1. Preheat oven to 350°. Wash chicken and season with salt and pepper. Heat oil in wok or frying pan. Add mushrooms and ginger. Stir-fry 2–3 minutes. Add green onions, and stir-fry 3–4 minutes. Stuff bird with mixture. Skewer it closed and tie legs together. Force wing tips back and under to form a stand. Place chicken in roasting pan.

2. Combine sugar, soy sauce, sherry, and broth. Pour over bird. Roast, basting often, for 1 1/4 hours. Let it sit 15 minutes. Carve bird and arrange on serving platter, with the stuffing under the meat.

3. Skim off fat from pan drippings. Heat 1 cup drippings in small pan. Stir cornstarch together with 2 Tbsp sherry. Stir into boiling drippings. Cook until clear and thickened. Pour over chicken or serve on the side.

Exchanges
3 Lean Meat

Calories 206
    Calories from Fat . . 71
Total Fat . . . . 8 g
    Saturated Fat . . . . . . 2 g
Cholesterol . . . . 72 mg
Sodium . . . . 362 mg
    W/o added salt . . . 229 mg
Carbohydrate . . . . 5 g
    Dietary Fiber . . . . . . 0 g
    Sugars . . . . 2 g
Protein . . . . 24 g

Haitian Banana Stuffed Chicken

Serves 8   Serving Size: 1/8 recipe

  1 Tbsp butter
  1 clove garlic, crushed
  1 cup soft bread cubes
     Juice and grated rind of 1 lime
  1 1/2 Tbsp rum
  1 tsp brown sugar
1/4 tsp nutmeg
     Dash hot pepper sauce
  1 tsp salt (optional)
     Freshly ground pepper
  3 bananas, peeled and chopped
  1 (4 1/2 lb) roasting chicken
     Nonfat cooking spray
  1 tsp allspice
  1 tsp nutmeg

1. Preheat oven to 350°. Heat butter in skillet. Add garlic and sauté 1–2 minutes, stirring. Remove from heat, add bread cubes, lime, rum, brown sugar, nutmeg, hot pepper sauce, salt, pepper, and bananas. Mix well.

2. Wash chicken. Stuff with mixture. Skewer it closed and tie legs together. Force wing tips back and under to form a stand.

3. Place in roasting pan on rack. Spray with cooking spray. Sprinkle on allspice and nutmeg. Roast 1 1/4 hours, spraying a few times with cooking spray. Let rest 15 minutes. Carve and arrange meat over stuffing to serve.

Exchanges
1 Fruit
5 Lean Meat

Calories 318
  Calories from Fat . . 99
Total Fat . . . . 11 g
  Saturated Fat . . . . . . 4 g
Cholesterol . . . . 119 mg
Sodium . . . . 408 mg
  W/o added salt . . . 175 mg
Carbohydrate . . . . . . 13 g
  Dietary Fiber . . . . . . 1 g
  Sugars . . . . 7 g
Protein . . . . 38 g

Roast Chicken with Apple Stuffing

Serves 8   Serving Size: 1/8 recipe

1 onion, chopped

1 stalk celery, chopped

4 cups peeled, cored, chopped apples

3 cups soft bread crumbs

2 Tbsp minced parsley

1 tsp salt (optional)

1/4 tsp pepper

1 tsp paprika

1/2 cup raisins

4 Tbsp butter, melted

1 (5 lb) roasting chicken, washed

1 Tbsp soy sauce

1. Preheat oven to 350°. Place first 9 ingredients (through raisins) in large bowl. Mix well. Mix in 3 Tbsp melted butter.

2. Stuff bird. Skewer closed. Cover leg ends with foil and tie together. Force wing tips back and under to form a stand. Place bird on rack in baking pan. Brush with 1 Tbsp butter and soy sauce. Bake 1 1/4–1 1/2 hours, or until a leg moves freely and juices run clear.

Exchanges

1 Starch	4 Lean Meat
1 Fruit	

Calories 440
  Calories from Fat   153
Total Fat . . . . 17 g
  Saturated Fat . . . . . . 7 g
Cholesterol . . . . 144 mg
Sodium . . . . 575 mg
  W/o added salt . . . 272 mg
Carbohydrate . . . . . . 28 g
  Dietary Fiber . . . . . . 3 g
  Sugars . . . . 19 g
Protein . . . . 43 g

Roast Chicken
with Dried Fruit Stuffing

Serves 8 Serving Size: 1/8 recipe

- 1/2 cup dried apricots
- 1/2 cup prunes
- 1 cup raisins
- 1 Tbsp canola oil
- 1 onion, chopped
- 2 stalks celery, chopped
- 1 (4–5 lb) roasting chicken
- Salt and pepper
- 2 Tbsp soy sauce
- Nonfat cooking spray

1. Put apricots, prunes, and raisins in bowl. Cover with hot water for 30 minutes. Drain.

2. Heat oil in skillet. Cook onion and celery until onion is limp. Mix into fruit. Preheat oven to 350°.

3. Wash chicken and season with salt and pepper. Stuff with fruit. Skewer closed. Wrap leg ends with foil and tie together. Force wing tips back and under to form a stand. Brush bird with soy sauce, then spray. Place on rack in baking pan. Roast 1 1/4 to 1 1/3 hours, or until a leg moves freely when jiggled. If breast browns too quickly, cover with foil. Let rest 10 minutes before carving.

Exchanges
1 Fruit
3 Lean Meat

Calories 244
  Calories from Fat . . 78
Total Fat . . . . 9 g
  Saturated Fat . . . . . . 2 g
Cholesterol . . . . 81 mg
Sodium . . . . 372 mg
  W/o added salt
  and 1/2 soy sauce 239 mg
Carbohydrate . . . . . . 14 g
  Dietary Fiber . . . . . . 2 g
  Sugars . . . . 8 g
Protein . . . . 27 g

Roast Chicken
with Garden Vegetables

Serves 8   Serving Size: 1/4 chicken + vegetables

- 2 (2 1/2 lb) chickens
- 1 tsp salt (optional)
- 1/4 tsp paprika
- Freshly ground pepper
- 6 celery tops
- 2 parsley sprigs
- 2 bay leaves
- 1 onion, quartered
- Nonfat cooking spray
- 2 Tbsp lite soy sauce
- 1/2 cup chopped fresh parsley
- 2 cloves garlic, crushed
- 1 onion, chopped
- 2 cups baby carrots
- 3 stalks celery, sliced
- 6 small new potatoes, or 3 large ones, quartered
- 2 Tbsp olive oil
- 1/2 tsp thyme
- 1/2 tsp salt (optional)
- Freshly ground pepper
- 1/2 lb asparagus, in 2-inch pieces

1. Preheat oven to 350°. Wash chickens. Put salt, paprika, and pepper into chicken cavities. Put 3 celery tops, 1 parsley sprig, 1 bay leaf, and 2 pieces of onion in each. Bend wing tips back and under to form a stand. Tie legs together. Spray baking dish and put chickens in dish. Brush birds with soy sauce and spray.

2. Mix parsley and garlic. Place onion, carrots, celery, and potatoes around chicken. Mix oil, thyme, salt, and pepper. Pour over vegetables and toss. Sprinkle with parsley-garlic mixture. Roast 45 minutes. Add asparagus. Roast 15–20 minutes. Place vegetables on heated platter and chicken, cut into quarters, on top.

Exchanges

1 Starch	4 Lean Meat
2 Vegetable	

Calories	408
Calories from Fat	135
Total Fat	15 g
Saturated Fat	3 g
Cholesterol	128 mg
Sodium	713 mg
W/o added salt . . .	239 mg
Carbohydrate	24 g
Dietary Fiber	3 g
Sugars	5 g
Protein	45 g

Roast Chicken with Plum Sauce

Serves 8   Serving Size: 1/8 recipe

- 1 (4–5 lb) roasting chicken
- Salt and pepper
- 2 sprigs fresh tarragon
- 1 Tbsp lite soy sauce
- Nonfat cooking spray
- 8 plums
- 1/2 cup water
- 1 onion, chopped
- 1 Tbsp butter
- Juice 1 lemon
- 1 tsp lite soy sauce
- 1/2 cup sugar
- 1 tsp Worcestershire sauce
- 1 Tbsp grated fresh ginger
- 1/4 tsp dry mustard

1. Preheat oven to 350°. Wash chicken. Season cavity with salt, pepper, and tarragon. Cover leg tips with foil, then tie together. Force wing tips back and under to form a stand.

2. Brush with soy sauce and spray. Place in baking dish on rack. Roast 1 1/4 hours, or until a leg moves freely when wiggled. Allow to rest 10 minutes before carving. Serve with sauce; recipe follows.

3. Cut plums in quarters, remove pits. Put in saucepan with 1/2 cup water. Bring to boil, cover, and simmer 15–20 minutes. Cool. Place in processor or blender and purée.

4. Sauté onion in butter. Add to plums in blender. Add remaining ingredients and puree. Heat sauce before serving.

Exchanges
1 1/2 Carbohydrate
4 Lean Meat

Calories 358
   Calories from Fat   108
Total Fat . . . . 12 g
   Saturated Fat . . . . . . 4 g
Cholesterol . . . . 119 mg
Sodium . . . . 300 mg
   W/o added salt . . . 234 mg
Carbohydrate . . . . . . 24 g
   Dietary Fiber . . . . . . 2 g
   Sugars . . . . 18 g
Protein . . . . 39 g

Rock Cornish Game Hens with Prune Stuffing

Serves 6   Serving Size: 1/2 (2 lb) bird, 1 (1 lb) bird

- 18 pitted prunes
- Dry sherry to cover prunes
- 6 (1 lb) cornish hens or 3 (2 lb) chickens
- 1 Tbsp canola oil
- Salt and pepper
- 2 Tbsp currant jelly
- 2 Tbsp sherry

1. Place prunes in bowl. Marinate in sherry overnight.

2. Preheat oven to 425°. Wash hens. Season cavities with salt and pepper. Drain prunes. Stuff 3 prunes in 1-lb hens or 6 prunes in 2-lb hens. Close with toothpicks. Tie legs together. Place in baking dish on rack. Brush with oil, salt, and pepper, and place in oven. Bake 25 minutes.

3. Melt jelly with 2 Tbsp sherry. Brush hens with glaze and bake 10 minutes. Repeat. Bake 45 minutes in all. If using 2-lb hens, cut in half down the middle. Arrange hens with 3 prunes under each half. Remove toothpicks and untie legs.

Exchanges
1 Fruit   1 Fat
4 Lean Meat

Calories 355
    Calories from Fat   149
Total Fat . . . . 17 g
    Saturated Fat . . . . . . 1 g
Cholesterol . . . . 52 mg
Sodium . . . . 245 mg
    W/o added salt . . . . 67 mg
Carbohydrate . . . . . . 23 g
    Dietary Fiber . . . . . . 2 g
    Sugars . . . . 16 g
Protein . . . . 28 g

Simple Roasted Planked Chicken

Serves 6   Serving Size: 1/6 recipe

1   (4 lb) roasting chicken

Nonfat cooking spray

1   tsp garlic powder

1   tsp ground tarragon

1   tsp ground thyme

1   tsp salt

Freshly ground pepper

1   Tbsp chopped fresh rosemary leaves

1/2   tsp paprika

Juice 1 lemon

1. Preheat oven to 375°. Wash chicken and split in half. Remove all fat. Remove backbone and reserve for making stock. Remove skin. Spray with cooking spray. Sprinkle with remaining ingredients, except lemon juice.

2. Spray baking dish. Lay chicken halves cut side down in dish. Squeeze lemon juice over chicken. Bake 40 minutes.

Exchanges

3 Lean Meat

Calories 188
Calories from Fat . . 65
Total Fat . . . . 7 g
Saturated Fat . . . . . . 2 g
Cholesterol . . . . 84 mg
Sodium . . . . 438 mg
W/o added salt . . . . 82 mg
Carbohydrate . . . . . . 3 g
Dietary Fiber . . . . . . 0 g
Sugars . . . . 0 g
Protein . . . . 28 g

Split Roasted Chicken on a Bed of Vegetables

Serves 6   Serving Size: 1/6 recipe

1	(4 lb) roasting chicken
2	sprigs fresh basil
2	sprigs fresh oregano
2	sprigs fresh thyme
	Nonfat cooking spray
1 1/2	cups chopped green onions
1	cup chopped celery
1	cup chopped mushrooms
2	small tomatoes, chopped
	Salt and pepper
1	Tbsp soy sauce

1. Preheat oven to 375°. Split chicken in half, removing backbone. Push 1 sprig of basil, oregano, and thyme between flesh and skin of each half of chicken.

2. Spray nonstick skillet with cooking spray. Add green onions, celery, and mushrooms. Sauté, stirring and spraying, 5 minutes. Add tomatoes and cook, stirring, 5 minutes. Salt and pepper to taste.

3. Put cooked vegetables in baking dish. Arrange chicken halves over vegetables, cut side down. Spray, then brush with soy sauce. Bake 45 minutes. Remove skin from chicken before serving.

Exchanges
4 Lean Meat

Calories 241
  Calories from Fat . . 76
Total Fat . . . . 8 g
  Saturated Fat . . . . . . 2 g
Cholesterol . . . . 96 mg
Sodium . . . . 399 mg
  W/o added salt . . . 220 mg
Carbohydrate . . . . . . 7 g
  Dietary Fiber . . . . . . 2 g
  Sugars . . . . 4 g
Protein . . . . 34 g

Rolled and Stuffed Chicken

This chapter has recipes for rolling and stuffing chicken scallops, boned legs and thighs, and various vegetables, such as peppers and onions, that can also be cooked with a filling.

Chicken Cordon Bleu

Serves 6   Serving Size: 1 roll and 1/4 cup sauce

Chicken:
- 3 boneless, skinless, chicken breasts, halved
- 1/4 lb gruyere or Swiss cheese
- 1/4 lb boiled ham, thinly sliced
- 1/4 cup egg substitute
- 1 cup dry bread crumbs
- 1/4 cup dried parsley flakes
- 1 tsp granulated garlic
- 1/2 tsp salt
- Freshly ground pepper
- Nonfat cooking spray
- 2 Tbsp canola oil

Sauce:
- 2 shallots, finely chopped
- 1 tsp juniper berries, crushed
- 4 Tbsp flour
- 2 cups low-sodium chicken broth, boiling
- 1/2 cup dry sherry
- Salt and pepper

1. Preheat oven to 350°. Place each chicken piece between 2 sheets wax paper and tap with mallet until flattened to 1/4 inch thick. Cut cheese into six 2 × 1/4 × 1/4-inch pieces. Lay one piece of ham on each chicken scallop. Place slice of cheese in center and roll up. Close with toothpicks.

2. Dip chicken in egg substitute. Mix bread crumbs with parsley, garlic, salt, and pepper. Roll chicken in mixture. Lay, seam side down, in sprayed baking dish. Bake 25 minutes.

3. Heat oil in pan. Add shallots and juniper berries. Sauté 2–3 minutes. Sprinkle with flour and cook, stirring, 2–3 minutes. Remove from heat

and pour on boiling broth, beating with whisk to prevent lumping. Return to heat and cook until thickened. Add sherry, salt, and pepper. Spoon over chicken rolls before serving.

Exchanges

2 1/2 Starch	1 1/2 Fat
5 Very Lean Meat	

Calories 381
  Calories from Fat . 127
Total Fat . . . . 14 g
  Saturated Fat . . . . . . 5 g
Cholesterol . . . . 99 mg
Sodium . . . . 613 mg
Carbohydrate . . . . . . 26 g
  Dietary Fiber . . . . . . 5 g
  Sugars . . . . 1 g
Protein . . . . 41 g

Stuffed Boned Chicken Legs

Serves 6   Serving Size: 1/6 recipe

        12 boneless, skinless chicken legs
         1 large carrot, scraped
         1 large onion
         1 green bell pepper
       1/4 lb mushrooms
            Nonfat cooking spray
         1 large apple, peeled and cored
         1 cup soft bread crumbs
         1 tsp salt (optional)
            Freshly ground pepper
         1 Tbsp chopped fresh tarragon
            Paprika
         2 cups low-sodium chicken broth
         1 Tbsp cornstarch
         2 Tbsp sherry

1. Preheat oven to 350°. Wash chicken legs and drain. Place carrot, onion, green bell pepper, and mushrooms in processor or blender and chop. Heat nonstick skillet. Spray with cooking spray, add vegetables, and cook, stirring, 5 minutes.

2. Place apple in processor and finely chop. Add to vegetables and cook, stirring 1–2 minutes. Spray again. Add bread crumbs, salt, pepper, and tarragon. Mix stuffing well.

3. Stuff chicken legs. Close with toothpicks. Place in baking dish. Sprinkle with paprika. Pour broth around legs. Bake, uncovered, 35–40 minutes. Remove legs from pan and keep warm.

4. Pour pan liquids through strainer into a pan. Bring to boil. Dissolve cornstarch in sherry. Stir into liquids. Cook until clear and thickened. Pour over chicken and serve.

Exchanges
1 Starch
4 Lean Meat

Calories 229
   Calories from Fat . . 54
Total Fat . . . . 6 g
   Saturated Fat . . . . . . 1 g
Cholesterol . . . . 82 mg
Sodium . . . . 487 mg
   W/o added salt . . . 132 mg
Carbohydrate . . . . . . 13 g
   Dietary Fiber . . . . . . 2 g
   Sugars . . . . 6 g
Protein . . . . 27 g

Stuffed Chicken Breasts Fundador

Serves 6   Serving Size: 1/6 recipe

3	skinless, boneless chicken breasts, halved
1	onion, chopped
1	Tbsp butter
1/4	lb mushrooms, chopped
2	Tbsp chopped fresh parsley
1	clove garlic, crushed
3	juniper berries, crushed
1	cup cooked brown rice
2	Tbsp grated Parmesan cheese
1/2	tsp salt (optional)
	Freshly ground pepper
1	Tbsp water
1/4	cup egg substitute
1	cup dry bread crumbs
	Nonfat cooking spray
2	shallots, chopped
1	Tbsp butter
2	Tbsp flour
1 1/2	cup chicken broth, boiling
1/4	cup white wine
1	Tbsp parsley, chopped
1/2	tsp salt (optional)
	Freshly ground pepper
1/4	cup evaporated fat-free milk
1/4	cup grated Parmesan cheese

1. Preheat oven to 350°. Place each breast half between 2 sheets wax paper or plastic wrap. Tap with a mallet until 1/4 inch thick. Sauté onion in butter until limp. Add mushrooms and cook 5 minutes. Add parsley, garlic, juniper berries, rice, cheese, salt, and pepper. Mix well. Place a spoonful of mixture on each chicken scallop. Roll up, and close with toothpicks.

2. Beat 1 Tbsp of water with egg substitute. Roll chicken in egg mixture, then in bread crumbs. Spray skillet. Add breasts and brown on each side.

3. Spray baking dish. Lay rolls seam side down in dish.

4. Sauté shallots in butter 1–2 minutes. Sprinkle with flour. Cook, stirring, 2–3 minutes. Remove from heat and add boiling broth, beating with whisk to prevent lumping. Return to heat and cook until thickened. Stir in wine, parsley, salt, pepper, and milk. Pour over chicken.

5. Sprinkle with Parmesan and bake 25–30 minutes.

Exchanges

1 1/2 Starch	1 Fat
1 Vegetable	
3 Very Lean Meat	

Calories 360
   Calories from Fat . . 63
Total Fat . . . . 10 g
   Saturated Fat . . . . . . 5 g
Cholesterol . . . . 88 mg
Sodium . . . . 747 mg
   W/o added salt . . . 392 mg
Carbohydrate . . . . . . 28 g
   Dietary Fiber . . . . . . 2 g
   Sugars . . . . 2 g
Protein . . . . 35 g

Herbed Stuffed Chicken Thighs with Mushrooms

Serves 6   Serving Size: 1/6 recipe

6	skinless, boneless chicken thighs
	Nonfat cooking spray
1/4	cup chopped green onions
1	clove garlic, crushed
1/4	cup finely chopped celery
1/4	cup each chopped red and green pepper
6	button mushrooms, finely chopped
1	sprig fresh thyme
1	sprig fresh cilantro
1/2	tsp salt (optional)
	Freshly ground pepper
1 1/2	cups fine dry bread crumbs
2	cups low-sodium chicken broth
1	Tbsp olive oil
1	large portobello mushroom, finely diced
2	Tbsp quick-mixing flour

1. Cover chicken with wax paper or plastic wrap and tap with mallet until flattened and twice as large. Preheat oven to 350°.

2. Spray skillet. Add green onions, garlic, celery, peppers, and button mushrooms. Cook, stirring, 5–6 minutes. Add thyme, cilantro, salt, and pepper. Cook 1 minute.

3. Place large spoonful of vegetable mixture in center of each thigh. Roll up and close with toothpicks. Spray each roll. Roll in bread crumbs. Spray baking dish with cooking spray and put thighs side by side in dish, seam side down. Bake, uncovered, 45 minutes.

4. Meanwhile, heat 2 cups chicken broth to boiling and reduce to 1 1/2 cups.

5. Put 1 Tbsp oil in skillet and remaining vegetables. Add portobello mushroom and cook 2–3 minutes. Sprinkle with flour and cook 1–2 minutes. Remove from heat and pour on boiling broth. Beat with whisk to prevent lumping. Return to heat and cook, stirring, until thickened. Pour over baked chicken and serve.

Exchanges
1 Starch
2 Lean Meat

Calories 185
  Calories from Fat . . 63
Total Fat . . . . 7 g
  Saturated Fat . . . . . 1.5 g
Cholesterol . . . . 37 mg
Sodium . . . . 309 mg
  W/o added salt . . . 175 mg
Carbohydrate . . . . . . 17 g
  Dietary Fiber . . . . . . 1 g
  Sugars . . . . 2 g
Protein . . . . 14 g

Chicken Birds

Serves 6   Serving Size: 1/6 recipe

1/2 lb mushrooms, finely chopped

1 small onion, finely chopped

2 Tbsp butter

2 Tbsp flour

1 cup low-sodium chicken broth, boiling

1/2 cup white wine

1/4 cup finely chopped cooked ham

1/2 cup bread crumbs

2 shallots, chopped

1 Tbsp chopped parsley

1 Tbsp chopped chives

1 egg yolk

1 Tbsp sherry

Salt and pepper

3 skinless, boneless chicken breasts, halved

Nonfat cooking spray

1 cup low-sodium chicken broth

1/2 cup white wine

1 tsp arrowroot

3 Tbsp white wine

2 Tbsp chopped parsley

1. Sauté mushrooms and onion in butter. Sprinkle with flour and cook, stirring, 2–3 minutes. Remove from heat and pour in broth, beating with whisk to prevent lumping. Add wine and cook, stirring often, 10 minutes. Add ham, bread crumbs, shallots, parsley, and chives. Stir in egg yolk, sherry, salt, and pepper.

2. Lay chicken between wax paper or plastic wrap and tap with mallet until 1/2 inch thick. Mound spoonful of stuffing in center of each. Roll up and close with toothpicks. Spray a pan. Add chicken and brown on all sides. Remove chicken.

3. Add broth to pan and cook, scraping up brown bits. Add wine. Cook until reduced by half. Add chicken to liquid. Cover and simmer 15–20 minutes. Remove chicken and keep warm. Mix arrowroot with wine. Stir into pan juices. Cook until clear and thickened. Pour over chicken, sprinkle with parsley, and serve.

(Freeze leftover stuffing in 2 Tbsp-size balls.)

Exchanges

1 Starch	1 Fat
1 Vegetable	
3 Very Lean Meat	

Calories 305
   Calories from Fat . . 81
Total Fat . . . . 9 g
   Saturated Fat . . . . . . 4 g
Cholesterol . . . . 121 mg
Sodium . . . . 447 mg
   W/o added salt . . . 269 mg
Carbohydrate . . . . . . 14 g
   Dietary Fiber . . . . . . 1 g
   Sugars . . . . 3 g
Protein . . . . 31 g

Chicken-Stuffed Cabbage Rolls

Serves 8   Serving Size: 1/8 recipe

1	large green cabbage
	Boiling water
1	Tbsp oil
1	onion, chopped
1	clove garlic, crushed
1	cup chopped mushrooms
1 1/2	lb ground chicken
1/2	cup egg substitute
1/4	cup fat-free milk
1	tsp salt (optional)
	Freshly ground pepper
1	tsp dried oregano, or 1 Tbsp chopped fresh
	Flour
2	Tbsp oil
1	carrot, sliced
1	onion, chopped
1	tomato, peeled, chopped
1/2	cup white wine
1	cup no-salt-added tomato sauce
1	tsp sugar
	Nonfat sour cream
	Chopped parsley

1. Cut core from cabbage. Remove 8 outer leaves. Remove white rib from center of each leaf. Put leaves in large pot. Pour boiling water to 1 inch over leaves. Cover and steam 2–3 minutes. Drain. Heat oil in skillet. Add onion and cook until limp. Add garlic and mushrooms. Cook 5 minutes, stirring.

2. Place chicken in bowl. Add egg substitute, fat-free milk, salt, pepper, and oregano. Add onion mixture. Mix well. Place spoonful of filling in center of cabbage leaf. Fold up and close with toothpicks. Roll in flour. Preheat oven to 350°.

3. Heat 2 Tbsp oil in skillet. Add cabbage rolls and brown. Remove and lay in casserole with a cover. Add carrot and onion to skillet. Sauté until onion is limp. Scatter over cabbage. Put tomatoes on top. Add wine, tomato sauce, and sugar. Bake, covered, for 1 hour. Uncover and bake 15 minutes. Serve with a dollop of sour cream and sprinkle with parsley.

Exchanges
1 Vegetable
3 Lean Meat

Calories 236
   Calories from Fat . . 63
Total Fat . . . . 7 g
   Saturated Fat . . . . . . 1 g
Cholesterol . . . . 52 mg
Sodium . . . . 370 mg
   W/o added salt . . . 103 mg
Carbohydrate . . . . . . 15 g
   Dietary Fiber . . . . . . 2 g
   Sugars . . . . 4 g
Protein . . . . 24 g

Chicken Pockets
with Spinach and Cheese

Serves 6   Serving Size: 1/6 recipe

1 onion, chopped

2 Tbsp oil

1 carrot, grated

1 clove garlic, crushed

1 sprig fresh thyme, or 1/4 tsp dried

1/2 lb fresh spinach, washed, stalks removed, chopped

1/2 tsp salt (optional)

1/8 tsp pepper

3 boneless, skinless chicken breasts, halved

1 1/2 cups dry bread crumbs

3 oz fat-free sharp cheddar cheese, grated

1 tsp granulated garlic

2 Tbsp dried parsley flakes

2 egg whites, beaten with 2 Tbsp water

Nonfat cooking spray

Paprika

1. Preheat oven to 350°. Sauté onion in oil until limp. Add carrot and cook 2–3 minutes. Add garlic, thyme, and spinach. Cover and cook until spinach wilts. Pour off excess water. Salt and pepper to taste. Allow to cool. Divide into 6 portions.

2. Cut pocket in side of each chicken half. Stuff each with spinach filling. Close with toothpicks.

3. Mix bread crumbs, cheese, garlic, and parsley flakes. Dip chicken in egg wash and roll in crumb mixture. Spray baking dish with cooking spray and put chicken pockets in. Spray chicken, sprinkle with paprika. Bake 30 minutes.

Exchanges

1 1/2 Starch	1/2 Fat
1 Vegetable	
4 Very Lean Meat	

Calories	313	
Calories from Fat	. . 81	
Total Fat	9	g
Saturated Fat	1	g
Cholesterol	73	mg
Sodium	581	mg
W/o added salt . . .	479	mg
Carbohydrate	24	g
Dietary Fiber	3	g
Sugars	3	g
Protein	33	g

Asparagus-Stuffed Chicken Scallops

Serves 8   Serving Size: 2 rolls

 4 boneless, skinless chicken breasts, halved
    Salt (optional)
    Freshly ground pepper
 1 lb asparagus spears, trimmed, cooked, cooled
1/2 lb reduced-fat sharp cheddar, thinly sliced
1/2 cup flour, divided
 1 tsp rosemary, crumbled
1/2 tsp salt (optional)
    Freshly ground pepper
 1 egg white beaten with 2 Tbsp water
 2 Tbsp canola oil
1/2 lb mushrooms, sliced
 1 small onion, chopped
 1 clove garlic, crushed
 2 cups low-sodium chicken broth, boiling

1. Cut each half breast in two, slicing from the side. Lay pieces between wax paper or plastic wrap and tap with mallet until 1/2-inch thick. Salt and pepper scallops to taste. Trim asparagus to fit scallop. Wrap asparagus with piece of cheese. Lay in center of scallop. Wrap and close with toothpick.

2. Mix half the flour with rosemary, salt, and pepper. Dip chicken in egg wash. Roll in flour. Pour 1 Tbsp oil into skillet. Heat to sizzling and add rolls. Brown on all sides. Remove and place in baking dish. Preheat oven to 350°.

3. Add 1 Tbsp oil to skillet. Add mushrooms and cook, stirring, 5 minutes. Remove. Add onion to skillet. Cook 2–3 minutes. Add garlic and cook 1 minute. Sprinkle with remaining flour. Cook, stirring, 2–3 minutes. Remove from heat, add boiling broth, beating with whisk. Cook, stirring, until thickened. Scatter mushrooms over chicken rolls. Pour sauce over all. Bake 30 minutes.

Exchanges

1/2 Starch	1 Fat
1 Vegetable	
4 Very Lean Meat	

Calories	268
Calories from Fat	. . 63
Total Fat	7 g
Saturated Fat	1 g
Cholesterol	73 mg
Sodium	488 mg
W/o added salt . . .	323 mg
Carbohydrate	14 g
Dietary Fiber	1 g
Sugars	1 g
Protein	35 g

Vidalia Onions
with Chicken Stuffing

Serves 6   Serving Size: 1 onion

6 medium Vidalia or Spanish onions
Boiling water
2 Tbsp oil
1/4 lb mushrooms, chopped
2 Tbsp finely chopped pimientos
1 lb ground chicken
1 tsp sage
1 tsp salt (optional)
Freshly ground pepper
1 cup soft bread crumbs
2 Tbsp chopped fresh parsley
Nonfat cooking oil
Paprika

1. Peel onions, cut flat surface off root end for onions to stand on. Stand in 6-quart Dutch oven. Pour in boiling water to reach half way up sides of onions. Bring to boil, cover, and simmer until crisp-tender when poked with sharp knife. Drain and cool. Remove centers of onions, leaving 1/2-inch shell. Chop centers.

2. Preheat oven to 350°. Heat oil in skillet. Add mushrooms and sauté 3–4 minutes. Add chopped onion and pimentos. Sauté 1 minute. Cool. Add chicken, sage, salt, pepper, bread crumbs, and parsley. Mix well. Divide into 6 portions. Stuff each onion. Spray baking dish. Arrange onions side by side in dish. Spray. Sprinkle with paprika. Bake for 35–40 minutes.

Exchanges
1 Starch
2 Lean Meat

Calories 192
    Calories from Fat . . 63
Total Fat . . . . 7 g
    Saturated Fat . . . . . . 1 g
Cholesterol . . . . 48 mg
Sodium . . . . 424 mg
    W/o added salt . . . . 69 mg
Carbohydrate . . . . . . 12 g
    Dietary Fiber . . . . . . 2 g
    Sugars . . . . 6 g
Protein . . . . 20 g

Chicken Salads and Cold Plates

This chapter includes cold chicken dishes with vegetables and condiments. Most are complete meals that can be served on hot summer days, on the patio or outdoor deck.

Chicken Pasta Salad

Serves 6   Serving Size: 1/6 recipe

1/2 cup light mayonnaise

1 Tbsp chopped fresh basil

2 tsp Dijon mustard

2 Tbsp cider vinegar

Freshly ground pepper

1/2 tsp salt (optional)

1 1/2 cups small pasta shells, cooked, drained

1 1/2 cups diced cooked chicken

1 cup frozen peas, thawed

3 stalks celery, chopped

1/2 red onion, thinly sliced

1 head Boston lettuce, washed, crisped

3 tomatoes, sliced

1 small cucumber, sliced

1/4 cup chopped fresh parsley

1. Mix mayonnaise, basil, mustard, vinegar, pepper, and salt. Place pasta in large bowl. Add chicken and toss. Mix in peas, celery, and onion. Add mayonnaise mixture and toss to mix. Chill before serving.

2. Arrange cups of lettuce around outside of large serving platter. Arrange tomato and cucumber slices on lettuce. Pile salad in center of plate. Sprinkle with parsley.

Exchanges

2 Starch   2 Lean Meat
1 Vegetable

Calories 290
    Calories from Fat . . 72
Total Fat . . . . 8 g
    Saturated Fat . . . . . . 1 g
Cholesterol . . . . 43 mg
Sodium . . . . 325 mg
    W/o added salt . . . 148 mg
Carbohydrate . . . . . . 33 g
    Dietary Fiber . . . . . . 2 g
    Sugars . . . . 7 g
Protein . . . . 21 g

Chicken Plate with Vegetables à la Greque

Serves 8 Serving Size: 1/8 recipe

24 asparagus spears, cooked, warm

1/2 cup low-fat or fat-free Italian dressing

24 thin slices cooked chicken

1 head Boston lettuce, washed, crisped

3 tomatoes, sliced

1 English cucumber, scored, thinly sliced

1 recipe Vegetables à la Greque, p. 202

1 recipe Strawberry Vinaigrette, p. 200

Fresh parsley, chopped

1. Place asparagus in bowl. Pour Italian dressing over all, cover, and marinate, turning occasionally, 4–6 hours.

2. Drain asparagus, put one on each chicken slice, and roll up. Arrange lettuce around outside of serving platter. Arrange chicken rolls, tomatoes, and sliced cucumber on lettuce cups, leaving center of platter free.

3. Mound drained vegetables à la Greque in center. Drizzle strawberry vinaigrette over chicken rolls. Sprinkle parsley over vegetables.

Exchanges

3 Vegetable   1 Fat
4 Very Lean Meat

Calories 275
   Calories from Fat . . 81
Total Fat . . . . 9 g
   Saturated Fat . . . . . . 2 g
Cholesterol . . . . 70 mg
Sodium . . . . 366 mg
   W/o added salt . . . 233 mg
Carbohydrate . . . . . . 17 g
   Dietary Fiber . . . . . . 4 g
   Sugars . . . . 10 g
Protein . . . . 31 g

Chicken, Potato, and Jicama Salad

Serves 8   Serving Size: 1/8 recipe

       1 cup low-sodium chicken broth
       1 lb skinless, boneless chicken breast
     1/2 tsp salt (optional)
     1/4 tsp white pepper
       2 red potatoes, unpeeled, diced
     1/4 cup lemon juice
    1 1/2 tsp olive oil
     1/2 cup light mayonnaise
     2/3 cup nonfat sour cream
       1 clove garlic, crushed
     1/3 cup chopped fresh chives
    1 1/2 cups jicama, peeled, diced
       1 cup peas, cooked, chilled
       1 head red romaine lettuce, washed, crisped
       4 tomatoes, sliced
       1 cup chopped fresh parsley

1. Place broth in deep skillet. Add chicken breast, bring to boil, cover and simmer 15 minutes. Remove chicken and drain. Cut into 1-inch cubes. Salt and pepper broth. Add potatoes, bring to boil, cover and simmer 15 minutes, or until potato is tender. Drain. Chill.

2. Combine lemon juice, olive oil, mayonnaise, sour cream, garlic, and chives. Beat with whisk. Mix in chicken, jicama, peas, and potatoes. Arrange lettuce leaves on platter. Lay tomato over lettuce and pile salad in the middle. Sprinkle with parsley and serve.

Exchanges
1 Starch	1 Fat
1 Vegetable	
2 Very Lean Meat	

Calories 218
  Calories from Fat . . 63
Total Fat . . . . 7 g
  Saturated Fat . . . . . . 1 g
Cholesterol . . . . 42 mg
Sodium . . . . 372 mg
  W/o added salt . . . 106 mg
Carbohydrate . . . . . . 21 g
  Dietary Fiber . . . . . . 3 g
  Sugars . . . . 4 g
Protein . . . . 19 g

Chicken Salad Plate with Vegetables

Serves 6   Serving Size: 1/6 recipe

3 boneless, skinless chicken breasts, halved

Water

1 tsp salt (optional)

5 peppercorns

2 large navel oranges

1 tsp Dijon mustard

1/2 tsp salt (optional)

1/8 tsp white pepper

3/4 cup fat-free mayonnaise

3 small zucchini

2 small yellow squash

Boiling water

2 Tbsp chopped fresh parsley

1. Place chicken in large pan in one layer. Cover with water. Add salt and peppercorns. Cover. Bring to boil, reduce heat to simmer, and poach 15–20 minutes. Remove from liquids, drain, and cool.

2. Grate zest (orange skin) of orange (1 1/2 Tbsp). Squeeze juice from oranges. Beat 1/4 cup juice, mustard, salt, pepper, and zest into mayonnaise.

3. Cut all squash into 1/4-inch rings. Place in pot and pour on boiling water. Blanch 30 seconds. Drain, then put into bowl of ice water. Drain well. Place in bowl. Add half mayonnaise mixture.

4. Cut chicken on diagonal, 3–4 slices each. Arrange slices on platter. Smooth remaining mayonnaise mixture on top. Surround with vegetables. Sprinkle on parsley. Keep chilled until serving.

Exchanges

1 Starch
1 Vegetable
3 Very Lean Meat

Calories 235
    Calories from Fat . . 32
Total Fat . . . . 4 g
    Saturated Fat . . . . . . 1 g
Cholesterol . . . . 73 mg
Sodium . . . . 650 mg
    W/o added salt . . . 473 mg
Carbohydrate . . . . . . 22 g
    Dietary Fiber . . . . . . 2 g
    Sugars . . . . 9 g
Protein . . . . 29 g

Chicken Garbanzo Tabouli

Serves 10   Serving Size: 1/10 recipe

2 cups bulgur
2 cups boiling water
2 cups diced cooked chicken
1 tomato, chopped
3 green onions, chopped
1 1-lb can garbanzo beans, drained, rinsed
1/2 cup chopped red bell pepper
1 carrot, grated
1/2 cup currants
1/4 cup chopped dried apricots
1/2 tsp salt (optional)
Freshly ground pepper
2 Tbsp chopped fresh basil
1/4 cup chopped fresh parsley
1/2 cup lemon juice
2 Tbsp olive oil
1 clove garlic, crushed
1/4 tsp cumin
1/2 tsp curry powder
1/2 tsp salt (optional)
Freshly ground pepper
6 leaves romaine lettuce, crisped

1. Place bulgur in bowl. Pour boiling water over and let stand until water has been absorbed (15–20 minutes). Cool.

2. Add chicken, tomato, green onions, garbanzo beans, bell pepper, carrot, currants, and apricots. Toss well. Sprinkle with salt, pepper, basil, and parsley.

3. Place lemon juice, oil, garlic, cumin, curry powder, salt, and pepper in screw-top jar and shake. Pour dressing over all and toss well. Arrange lettuce on serving platter. Heap bulgur in middle and serve.

Exchanges

2 Starch	1 Lean Meat
1 Fruit	

Calories 260
  Calories from Fat . . 54
Total Fat . . . . 6 g
  Saturated Fat . . . . . . 1 g
Cholesterol . . . . 24 mg
Sodium . . . . 463 mg
  W/o added salt . . . 250 mg
Carbohydrate . . . . . . 40 g
  Dietary Fiber . . . . . 10 g
  Sugars . . . . 3 g
Protein . . . . 15 g

Elegant Chicken Breast in Aspic with Strawberry Vinaigrette

Serves 6   Serving Size: 1/6 recipe

Vinaigrette:
- 1 cup chopped fresh strawberries
- Freshly ground pepper
- 2 Tbsp balsamic vinegar
- 2 tsp sugar
- 1 Tbsp oil
- 2 Tbsp water

Aspic:
- 3 cups low-sodium chicken broth
- 1 cup no-salt-added tomato juice
- 4 envelopes unflavored gelatin
- 1 tsp sugar
- 2 egg whites
- 2 egg shells
- 1/4 cup sherry

Salad:
- 3 boneless, skinless chicken breasts, halved, poached drained, p. 197
- 6 basil leaves
- 6 cups torn lettuce leaves
- 3 tomatoes, sliced
- 1 English cucumber, unpeeled, scored, sliced

1. Place strawberries, pepper, vinegar, sugar, oil, and water in food processor or blender. Puree. Makes 3/4 cup vinaigrette. To make aspic, place ingredients from chicken broth to egg shells in saucepan. Bring to boil, stirring. Strain through several layers of damp cheesecloth. Stir in sherry.

2. Place chicken on plate. Lay basil leaf on each. Pour thin layer of aspic in bottom of jelly roll pan. Chill. Arrange breasts in pan. Spoon aspic over chicken. Chill. Spoon another layer of aspic over chicken. Chill. Repeat. Refrigerate until very firm.

3. Arrange lettuce around platter. Arrange tomato and cucumber on lettuce. Cut around edges of aspic-coated chicken breast. Heat spatula by dipping in hot water. Slide under each chicken. Place in center of platter. Drizzle vinaigrette over lettuce, tomatoes, and cucumber. Chop remaining aspic and scatter around edges of chicken. Serve.

Exchanges

1 Carbohydrate   1/2 Fat
5 Very Lean Meat

Calories 286	
Calories from Fat . . 54	
Total Fat . . . . 6 g	
Saturated Fat . . . . . . 1 g	
Cholesterol . . . . 73 mg	
Sodium . . . . 138 mg	
Carbohydrate . . . . . . 18 g	
Dietary Fiber . . . . . . 3 g	
Sugars . . . . 10 g	
Protein . . . . 37 g	

Herbed Yogurt Chicken with Vegetables à la Greque

Serves 8   Serving Size: 1/8 recipe

Vegetables:
- 1 cup chopped fennel
- 1 cup chopped celery
- 1/2 cup chopped green bell pepper
- 1/2 cup chopped red bell pepper
- 1 onion, sliced
- 1 cup thinly sliced carrots
- 1 cup broccoli florets
- Juice of 1 1/2 lemons
- 2 Tbsp olive oil
- Freshly ground pepper
- 1/2 tsp ground coriander
- Pinch thyme
- 1/2 tsp salt (optional)
- 2 cups water
- 1 cup slivered zucchini

1. Place fennel, celery, peppers, onion, carrot, and broccoli in pot. Mix lemon juice, olive oil, pepper, coriander, thyme, salt, and water. Pour over vegetables, bring to boil, cover, and simmer 10 minutes. Add zucchini, remove from heat, cover, and cool in liquid.

Chicken: 3   boneless, skinless chicken breasts, halved

1   bay leaf

1   sprig parsley

1   celery top

1   onion, coarsely chopped

1/2   tsp salt (optional)

4–5   peppercorns

2   cups plain yogurt

1/2   tsp cumin

1   Tbsp each chopped fresh mint, dill, parsley, and tarragon

1/2   Tbsp chopped fresh rosemary

2   Tbsp maple syrup

1   tsp salt and freshly ground pepper

1   head romaine lettuce, washed, crisped

1. Put chicken in skillet. Add bay leaf, parsley, celery top, and onion. Cover with water. Add salt and peppercorns. Bring to boil, reduce heat, and simmer 12–15 minutes, or until chicken resists pressure. Drain, cool, and slice diagonally.

2. Put yogurt in bowl. Add ingredients from cumin to pepper. Mix well. Pour over chicken. Refrigerate for at least 4 hours.

3. Arrange lettuce on platter. Place drained vegetables in center and chicken on top.

Exchanges

3 Vegetable   1 Fat
2 Very Lean Meat

Calories 185
    Calories from Fat . . 54
Total Fat . . . . 6 g
    Saturated Fat . . . . . . 1 g
Cholesterol . . . . 36 mg
Sodium . . . . 633 mg
    W/o added salt . . . 100 mg
Carbohydrate . . . . . . 17 g
    Dietary Fiber . . . . . . 2 g
    Sugars . . . . 6 g
Protein . . . . 16 g

Curried Chicken Salad

If you want a hot, spicy salad, increase the curry powder to 1 Tbsp.

Serves 6   Serving Size: 1/6 recipe

1/3	cup light mayonnaise
1/3	cup plain yogurt
2	tsp curry powder
1	tsp granulated garlic
3	cups diced cooked chicken
1 1/2	cup diced cantaloupe
1/4	cup raisins
1	Tbsp chopped cashew nuts
1/4	cup chopped fresh parsley

1. In bowl, mix mayonnaise, yogurt, curry powder, and garlic.

2. Add chicken, cantaloupe, raisins, cashews, and parsley. Mix well. Allow to rest 30 minutes in the refrigerator before serving.

Exchanges

1 Fruit	1 Fat
3 Very Lean Meat	

Calories 198
   Calories from Fat . . 54
Total Fat . . . . 6 g
   Saturated Fat . . . . . . 1 g
Cholesterol . . . . 53 mg
Sodium . . . . 80 mg
Carbohydrate . . . . . . 15 g
   Dietary Fiber . . . . . . 1 g
   Sugars . . . . 11 g
Protein . . . . 20 g

Chicken Rolls with Tuna Dressing

Serves 8 Serving Size: 1/8 recipe

1	cup boiling water
1/2	oz sun-dried tomatoes (about 15)
3/4	cup tomatoes, diced, peeled, seeded
1	Tbsp chopped fresh chives
1	6-oz can water-packed tuna
1/2	cup nonfat ranch dressing
1	Tbsp Dijon mustard
	Freshly ground pepper
1	Tbsp capers
1 1/2	lb cooked chicken, in 1/8-inch slices
	Romaine lettuce, washed, crisped
8	lemon wedges

1. In small bowl, pour boiling water over tomatoes and let sit 5 minutes. Drain and chop. Mix with fresh tomatoes. Sprinkle with chives and toss.

2. Place undrained tuna in processor or blender. Add salad dressing, mustard, and pepper. Puree. If too thick, add a little water. Stir in capers.

3. Roll 24 slices of chicken into tubes.
Arrange lettuce on platter.
Place chicken rolls on lettuce.
Pour tuna sauce over chicken.
Sprinkle with tomato mixture. Put
lemon wedges around edge.

Exchanges

1 Vegetable	1/2 Fat
3 Very Lean Meat	

Calories 164	
Calories from Fat . . 27	
Total Fat . . . . 3 g	
Saturated Fat . . . . . . 1 g	
Cholesterol . . . . 56 mg	
Sodium . . . . 372 mg	
Carbohydrate . . . . 8 g	
Dietary Fiber . . . . . . 1 g	
Sugars . . . . 1 g	
Protein . . . . 26 g	

Chicken Soups

Chicken soup has a great reputation as a cure-all for any number of ailments. This may not be a proven fact, but chicken soup is comforting nourishment for someone who is ill.

Bahamian Chicken Vegetable Soup

Serves 12   Serving Size: 1 cup

1 (3 1/2 lb) chicken
8 cups low-sodium beef broth
2 cups no-salt-added canned tomatoes
1 large onion, chopped
2 medium yams or sweet potatoes, peeled, cubed
2 medium potatoes, cubed, skins on
1 cup winter squash, cubed and peeled (hubbard or acorn)
2 cups frozen corn kernels
1/2 cup peas, frozen or fresh
1 jalapeño pepper, seeded, chopped
2 tsp salt (optional)
2 Tbsp chopped fresh chives

1. Place chicken in pot. Add beef broth, tomatoes, and onion. Bring to boil, reduce heat, and simmer 45 minutes. Cool, leaving chicken in liquids. Remove chicken, and cover chicken and pot with plastic wrap. Refrigerate overnight.

2. Remove hardened fat from liquids. Remove chicken skin and chop the meat to make 2 cups. (Leftover chicken can be used in other dishes.)

3. Bring liquids to boil. Add all remaining ingredients except chives. Bring to boil and cook 10 minutes. Add chicken. Cook 10 minutes. Sprinkle with chives before serving.

Exchanges

1 1/2 Starch	1/2 Fat
2 Very Lean Meat	

Calories 220
    Calories from Fat . . 45
Total Fat . . . . 5 g
    Saturated Fat . . . . . . 1 g
Cholesterol . . . . 54 mg
Sodium . . . . 456 mg
    W/o added salt . . . 101 mg
Carbohydrate . . . . . . 24 g
    Dietary Fiber . . . . . . 2 g
    Sugars . . . . 4 g
Protein . . . . 21 g

Cream of Chicken Soup

Serves 10   Serving Size: 1 cup

1	(3 1/2 lb) chicken, quartered
1	large onion, chopped
2	stalks celery
1	cup diced carrots
1	tsp salt (optional)
1/2	tsp white pepper
6	cups water
2	red potatoes, skins on, diced
1/3	cup quick-mixing flour
1/2	cup fat-free milk
1	12 oz-can evaporated fat-free milk, scalded
1/4	cup chopped chives, fresh or dried

1. Place chicken, onion, celery, carrots, salt, pepper, and water in pot. Bring to boil, cover, and reduce heat. Simmer 1 1/2 hours. Remove chicken from broth. Strain liquids, reserving vegetables.

2. Place broth in refrigerator until fat has hardened. Remove fat. Remove skin from chicken. Chop meat. Bring broth to boil. Add potatoes and cook 10–15 minutes. Add reserved vegetables. Add chicken. Beat flour into 1/2 cup milk. Add evaporated milk. Stir in flour-milk mixture. Cook 10 minutes. Stir in chives.

Exchanges

1 Starch	1/2 Fat
3 Very Lean Meat	

Calories 220
 Calories from Fat . . 45
Total Fat . . . . 5 g
 Saturated Fat . . . . . . 2 g
Cholesterol . . . . 66 mg
Sodium . . . . 331 mg
 W/o added salt . . . 119 mg
Carbohydrate . . . . . . 16 g
 Dietary Fiber . . . . . . 1 g
 Sugars . . . . 1 g
Protein . . . . 26 g

Traditional Chicken Noodle Soup

Serves 10 Serving Size: 1 cup

1 (4–5 lb) chicken, skin and fat removed
Cold water
1 large onion, chopped
2 carrots, peeled, chopped
2 stalks celery, chopped
1 tsp salt (optional)
1/2 tsp white pepper
2 cups broad noodles
1/4 cup chopped fresh parsley

1. Place chicken in pot. Cover with cold water. Add onion, carrots, celery, salt, and pepper. Bring to boil, lower heat to simmer, cover, and cook 1 1/2 hours.

2. Remove chicken from broth. Remove flesh from bones, chop, cover with plastic wrap, and refrigerate. Refrigerate broth overnight. Remove hardened fat. Remove carrots from soup, mash, and return to soup. Bring to boil.

3. Add noodles to soup and cook 6–8 minutes. Add chicken and parsley. Heat. Serve.

Exchanges
1 Starch
3 Lean Meat

Calories 235
   Calories from Fat . . 51
Total Fat . . . . 6 g
   Saturated Fat . . . . . . 1 g
Cholesterol . . . . 65 mg
Sodium . . . . 421 mg
   W/o added salt . . . 208 mg
Carbohydrate . . . . . . 20 g
   Dietary Fiber . . . . . . 2 g
   Sugars . . . . 2 g
Protein . . . . 25 g

Simple Chicken Consommé

Serves 12 Serving Size: 1 cup

    1 (4–5 lb) chicken, cut in quarters
  1/2 lb round steak, cubed
    2 carrots, peeled, chopped
  1/4 yellow turnip, peeled, chopped
    1 leek, cleaned, chopped
    2 stalks celery, chopped
    1 onion, chopped
    1 clove garlic, crushed
    1 bay leaf
    1 sprig thyme
    1 tsp salt (optional)
    8 peppercorns
    1 raw egg white beaten and egg shell

1. Place all ingredients except egg white and shell in large pot. Cover with 4 quarts water. Bring to boil. Cover and simmer 2 1/2–3 hours. Remove chicken and beef. Use for another purpose.

2. Strain broth through 2 layers of damp cheesecloth. Discard vegetables. Refrigerate broth. When fat is hard, remove and discard. To clarify broth, bring to boil. If too mild, reduce over high heat, uncovered, until desired strength.

3. Add egg white and crushed shell to boiling broth. Cook 10 minutes. Strain through 2 layers of wet cheesecloth. Can be frozen in 1-cup portions.

Exchanges
1/2 Carbohydrate

Calories 37
  Calories from Fat . . . 9
Total Fat . . . . 1 g
  Saturated Fat . . . . . . 0 g
Cholesterol . . . . 0 mg
Sodium . . . . 201 mg
  W/o added salt . . . . 62 mg
Carbohydrate . . . . 5 g
  Dietary Fiber . . . . . . 1 g
  Sugars . . . . 1 g
Protein . . . . 3 g

Cream of Leek and Watercress Soup

Serves 10   Serving Size: 1 cup

  1 Tbsp butter
  2 leeks, well washed, chopped
  2 potatoes, peeled, diced
  4 cups low-sodium chicken broth
1/2 tsp each nutmeg and mace
  1 tsp salt (optional)
1/4 tsp white pepper
  3 cups fat-free milk
  3 Tbsp quick-mixing flour
  1 cup chopped watercress
  1 cup chopped cooked chicken

1. Heat butter in saucepan. Add leeks and potato. Sauté 5 minutes, stirring. Add broth, nutmeg, mace, salt, and pepper. Bring to boil. Reduce heat and simmer 20 minutes. Cool, then puree in blender or processor. Return to pan.

2. Beat fat-free milk into flour to make smooth paste. Stir into soup, with watercress and chicken. Cook 10 minutes, stirring often.

Exchanges
1 Starch
1 Lean Meat

Calories 139
  Calories from Fat . . 18
Total Fat . . . . 2 g
  Saturated Fat . . . . . . 1 g
Cholesterol . . . . 19 mg
Sodium . . . . 309 mg
  W/o added salt . . . . 96 mg
Carbohydrate . . . . . . 19 g
  Dietary Fiber . . . . . . 1 g
  Sugars . . . . 4 g
Protein . . . . 10 g

Pot-au-Feu

Serves 10   Serving Size: 1 cup

Make simple consommé, p. 210. Remove all meat from chicken and chop.
Chop steak. Set aside. Clarify consommé. Use 8 cups of broth and freeze
the rest.

8	cups consommé
1	onion, chopped
2	carrots, chopped
1	leek, washed, chopped
1	stalk celery, chopped
2	cups shredded cabbage
1/2	lb vermicelli
1	cup frozen peas
1/2	cup chopped fresh parsley
	Chicken, chopped
	Beef, chopped

1. Place consommé, onion, carrots, leek, celery, and cabbage in stockpot.
   Bring to boil, cover, and simmer 30 minutes.

2. Add vermicelli and cook 7 minutes.
   Add peas, parsley, chicken, and beef.
   Heat thoroughly.

Exchanges
4 Lean Meat
2 Starch

Calories 295
   Calories from Fat . . 63
Total Fat . . . . 7 g
   Saturated Fat . . . . . . 2 g
Cholesterol . . . . 78 mg
Sodium . . . . 295 mg
   W/o added salt . . . 118 mg
Carbohydrate . . . . . . 26 g
   Dietary Fiber . . . . . . 2 g
   Sugars . . . . 5 g
Protein . . . . 36 g

Chicken Gumbo

Serves 10　Serving Size: 1 1/2 cups

　　1　(4–5 lb) chicken, cut in pieces, skin and fat removed
　　2　Tbsp flour
　　2　Tbsp oil
　　1　large onion, chopped
　　1　cup celery, chopped
　　6　cups water
　　1　tsp salt (optional)
　　　　Freshly ground pepper
　　1　cup diced carrots
　　1　28-oz can crushed tomatoes
　　1　tsp cumin
　1/2　tsp ground coriander
　1/2　tsp cayenne
　1/2　cup frozen corn niblets
1 1/2　cups red potatoes, skins on, diced
　　2　10-oz pkg frozen okra
　　1　sprig fresh thyme
　1/4　cup chopped fresh parsley

1. Dredge chicken in flour. Heat oil in large pot. Brown chicken on all sides. Remove.

2. Add onion to pot and cook, stirring, until limp. Add celery and cook, stirring, 3 minutes.

3. Return chicken to pot. Add water, salt, pepper, carrots, and tomatoes. Bring to boil, cover, and simmer 1 hour.

4. Remove chicken, cut meat from bones, and dice. Add to soup with cumin, coriander, cayenne, corn, potatoes, okra, and thyme. Simmer 30 minutes. Stir in parsley and serve.

Exchanges

1 Starch	3 Lean Meat
2 Vegetable	

Calories 309
   Calories from Fat . . 90
Total Fat . . . . 10 g
   Saturated Fat . . . . . . 2 g
Cholesterol . . . . 83 mg
Sodium . . . . 737 mg
   W/o added salt . . . 496 mg
Carbohydrate . . . . . . 23 g
   Dietary Fiber . . . . . . 3 g
   Sugars . . . . 5 g
Protein . . . . 31 g

Senegalese Soup

Serves 8   Serving Size: 1 cup

  1 Tbsp butter

  1 onion, chopped

  1 stalk celery, chopped

  1 apple, peeled, cored, chopped

  2 Tbsp flour

  2 tsp curry powder

  6 cups low-sodium chicken broth, boiling

  1 bay leaf

12 oz ice-cold evaporated milk, lightly whipped

  1 cup chopped chicken

1. Melt butter in saucepan. Cook onion and celery until onion is limp. Add apple and cook 1–2 minutes. Sprinkle with flour and curry powder. Cook, stirring, 2–3 minutes.

2. Remove from heat and add boiling broth. Beat with whisk to prevent lumping. Add bay leaf. Return to heat and simmer 15 minutes, covered. Stir occasionally. Remove and discard bay leaf.

3. Cool, then puree in blender or processor. Chill. Fold whipped evaporated milk and chicken into soup. Serve at once.

Exchanges
1 Carbohydrate
1 Lean Meat

Calories 138
   Calories from Fat . . 27
Total Fat . . . . 3 g
   Saturated Fat . . . . . . 1 g
Cholesterol . . . . 27 mg
Sodium . . . . 142 mg
Carbohydrate . . . . . . 13 g
   Dietary Fiber . . . . . . 1 g
   Sugars . . . . 3 g
Protein . . . . 14 g

Chicken Stir-Fry Dishes

Stir-frying is one of the fastest and healthiest methods of cooking. It can be done easily in an electric frying pan or a wok. A wok is an inexpensive cooking utensil that would be a great addition to your kitchen. The high sides and limited cooking surface make only very small amounts of oil necessary. A wok is perfect for quick cooking. If you are purchasing one for the first time, consider a nonstick surface. Most of these stir-fry recipes are served with plain boiled rice, but you can substitute cooked hot pasta.

Chicken Stir-Fry #1

Serves 4   Serving Size: 1/4 recipe

6 dried shitake mushrooms
1 boneless, skinless chicken breast
2 Tbsp grated fresh ginger
1 green onion, finely chopped
1 Tbsp sherry
1 Tbsp lite soy sauce
Pinch sugar
1 Tbsp canola oil
1/2 cup canned bamboo shoots, drained
2 Tbsp chopped walnut meats
1 Tbsp cornstarch
1/2 cup low-sodium chicken broth

1. Soak mushrooms 30 minutes in warm water. Drain and chop. Cut chicken into 1/2 × 2-inch strips. Place in bowl. Mix ginger, onion, sherry, soy sauce, and sugar. Pour over chicken and marinate 15 minutes, turning occasionally. Remove chicken and reserve liquid.

2. Heat oil in wok or frying pan. Cook chicken until no longer pink. Push chicken to side and add mushrooms. Cook, stirring, 2–3 minutes. Add bamboo shoots and walnuts.

3. Pour reserved marinade over all. Mix cornstarch with cold chicken broth. Stir into wok. Cook until clear and thickened.

Exchanges

1/2 Starch	1 Fat
2 Very Lean Meat	

Calories 154
    Calories from Fat . . 54
Total Fat . . . . 6 g
    Saturated Fat . . . . . . 1 g
Cholesterol . . . . 37 mg
Sodium . . . . 192 mg
Carbohydrate . . . . 8 g
    Dietary Fiber . . . . . . 1 g
    Sugars . . . . 1 g
Protein . . . . 15 g

Chicken Stir-Fry #2

Serves 4   Serving Size: 1/4 recipe

> 1 boneless, skinless chicken breast
> 1/2 lb asparagus
> 2 Tbsp sherry
> 1 Tbsp lite soy sauce
> 1/2 tsp sugar
> 1 Tbsp canola oil
> 1 onion, thinly sliced
> 1 clove garlic, crushed
> 2 Tbsp grated fresh ginger
> 1/2 cup canned bamboo shoots, drained
> 1/2 cup chicken broth
> 1 Tbsp cornstarch
> 1 cup fresh or canned bean sprouts, rinsed

1. Cut chicken breast in thin strips. Hold asparagus spear at each end and bend until tough stalk snaps off. Cut upper portion into 1-inch pieces. Mix sherry, soy sauce, and sugar, and marinate chicken 15 minutes. Drain, reserving liquid.

2. Heat oil in wok or electric frying pan. Add onion and cook until limp. Add garlic and ginger. Add asparagus and cook, stirring, 3–4 minutes. Add chicken and cook, stirring, 4–5 minutes. Add bamboo shoots.

3. Mix cold broth with cornstarch and stir until dissolved. Mix with sherry marinade. Pour over chicken and vegetables. Cook until thickened and clear. Stir in bean sprouts and heat through.

Exchanges

2 Vegetable	1 Fat
2 Very Lean Meat	

Calories 186
  Calories from Fat . . 45
Total Fat . . . . 5 g
  Saturated Fat . . . . . . 1 g
Cholesterol . . . . 37 mg
Sodium . . . . 202 mg
Carbohydrate . . . . . . 13 g
  Dietary Fiber . . . . . . 1 g
  Sugars . . . . 2 g
Protein . . . . 18 g

Chicken Stir-Fry à l'Orange

Serves 4   Serving Size: 1/4 recipe

- 1 tsp grated orange peel
- 3/4 cup orange juice
- 1 Tbsp lite soy sauce
- 1 Tbsp cornstarch
- 1 tsp low-sodium chicken boullion granules
- Freshly ground pepper
- Nonfat cooking spray
- 1 onion, sliced
- 2 boneless, skinless chicken breasts, cubed
- 1 clove garlic, crushed
- 1/4 lb mushrooms, sliced
- 1 red bell pepper, seeded, chopped

1. Mix first 6 ingredients together.

2. Spray wok or frying pan with cooking spray. Add onion and cook, stirring, until limp. Add chicken and garlic. Spray again. Cook until chicken is no longer pink. Add mushrooms and red pepper. Cook 4–5 minutes. Add orange juice mixture and cook until clear and thickened.

Exchanges
1 Carbohydrate
4 Very Lean Meat

Calories 205
  Calories from Fat . . 36
Total Fat . . . . 4 g
  Saturated Fat . . . . . . 1 g
Cholesterol . . . . 73 mg
Sodium . . . . 216 mg
Carbohydrate . . . . . . 14 g
  Dietary Fiber . . . . . . 2 g
  Sugars . . . . 7 g
Protein . . . . 29 g

Stir-Fry Chicken, Tomatoes, and Zucchini

Serves 4 Serving Size: 1/4 recipe

 2 cups low-sodium chicken broth
 1 cup long-grain rice
 1 boneless, skinless chicken breast, cubed
 1 Tbsp lite soy sauce
 1 Tbsp sherry
 2 Tbsp canola oil
 1 onion, chopped
 1 Tbsp cornstarch
 1/2 cup low-sodium chicken broth
 1 tsp sugar
 1 Tbsp lite soy sauce
 2 tomatoes, peeled, seeded, chopped
 1 zucchini, slivered

1. Bring chicken broth to boil. Add rice, reduce heat, cover and simmer 20 minutes. Fluff with fork and keep warm. Place chicken in bowl. Mix soy sauce and sherry. Pour over chicken, and marinate 15 minutes.

2. Drain chicken, reserving liquid. Heat oil in a wok. Add onion and cook until limp. Add chicken and cook 2–3 minutes. Mix reserved liquid with cornstarch and add to chicken broth, sugar, and soy sauce. Pour into wok. Stir-fry 2–3 minutes. Add tomatoes and zucchini. Stir-fry 2–3 minutes or until vegetables are warmed. Serve over rice.

Exchanges

3 Starch 1 Vegetable
1 Fat   2 Very Lean Meat

Calories 378
  Calories from Fat . . 81
Total Fat . . . . 9 g
  Saturated Fat . . . . . . 1 g
Cholesterol . . . . 37 mg
Sodium . . . . 386 mg
  With 1 Tbsp
    soy sauce . . . . . . 237 mg
Carbohydrate . . . . . . 50 g
  Dietary Fiber . . . . . . 2 g
  Sugars . . . . 6 g
Protein . . . . 21 g

Stir-Fry Chicken and Scallops

Serves 6   Serving Size: 1/6 recipe

4	dried shiitake mushrooms
1/2	lb small bay scallops
1	boneless, skinless chicken breast, in thin strips
1/2	cup white wine
2	Tbsp lite soy sauce
	Freshly ground pepper
1	small onion, grated
2	Tbsp canola oil
3	green onions, chopped
1	clove garlic, crushed
1/2	red bell pepper, finely chopped
1/2	cup sliced canned water chestnuts
1	Tbsp cornstarch
1	tsp low-sodium chicken bouillon granules

1. Soak mushrooms in hot water 30 minutes. Drain and chop. Place scallops and chicken in bowl. Mix wine, soy sauce, pepper, and onion. Marinate scallops and chicken 1 hour. Drain and reserve liquids.

2. Heat oil in wok. Stir-fry chicken and scallops 5 minutes. Remove. Add green onions, garlic, mushrooms, and pepper to wok. Stir-fry 1–2 minutes. Return chicken and scallops to wok. Stir-fry 3–4 minutes. Add water chestnuts.

3. Mix reserved marinade with cornstarch and bouillon. Pour over chicken and scallops. Cook, stirring, until clear and thickened. Serve at once.

Exchanges

1 Vegetable	1 Fat
2 Very Lean Meat	

Calories 168
 Calories from Fat . . 54
Total Fat . . . . 6 g
 Saturated Fat . . . . . . 1 g
Cholesterol . . . . 37 mg
Sodium . . . . 285 mg
Carbohydrate . . . . 8 g
 Dietary Fiber . . . . . . 1 g
 Sugars . . . . 1 g
Protein . . . . 17 g

Stir-Fry Szechwan Chicken with Eggplant

Szechwan cuisine is very peppery. If you prefer mild heat, use only one chili pepper.

Serves 4   Serving Size: 1/4 recipe

- 1 boneless, skinless chicken breast, in thin strips
- 1 Tbsp cornstarch
- 1 Tbsp lite soy sauce
- 1 Tbsp sherry
- 1 eggplant, peeled
  Boiling water
- 2 jalapeño chilis
- 2 Tbsp oil
- 2 Tbsp grated fresh ginger
- 1 clove garlic, crushed
- 1/4 cup low-sodium chicken broth

1. Place chicken in bowl. Mix cornstarch, soy sauce, and sherry, and toss with chicken. Cut eggplant into strips. Boil 3 cups water in pan. Add eggplant and par-boil 5 minutes. Drain well. Using rubber gloves, seed and chop jalapeños.

2. Heat 1 Tbsp oil in wok. Add jalapeños and stir-fry 1–2 minutes. Remove from wok. Heat remaining oil, add chicken, and stir-fry 1–2 minutes. Add ginger and garlic. Stir-fry 1–2 minutes.

3. Add broth, eggplant, and chili peppers. Stir-fry 1–2 minutes. Serve with soy sauce.

Exchanges

1 Starch	1 Fat
2 Very Lean Meat	

Calories 193
  Calories from Fat . . 81
Total Fat . . . . 9 g
  Saturated Fat . . . . . . 1 g
Cholesterol . . . . 37 mg
Sodium . . . . 397 mg
Carbohydrate . . . . . . 11 g
  Dietary Fiber . . . . . . 0 g
  Sugars . . . . 0 g
Protein . . . . 15 g

Teriyaki Chicken Scallops

Serves 4   Serving Size: 1/4 recipe

    2 boneless, skinless chicken breasts, halved
    3 Tbsp dry sherry
    3 Tbsp lite soy sauce
1 1/2 Tbsp honey
    1 clove garlic, crushed
    1 Tbsp grated fresh ginger
    1 Tbsp canola oil
    1 Tbsp cornstarch

1. Place chicken between two sheets of wax paper and tap with mallet until chicken is 1/4 inch thick. Mix sherry, soy sauce, honey, garlic, and ginger, and marinate chicken 15–20 minutes. Drain chicken, reserving liquid.

2. Heat oil in nonstick skillet or wok. Add chicken and sauté quickly on each side, about 6 minutes. Mix cornstarch with reserved liquid. Pour over chicken and cook until clear and thickened. Serve at once.

Exchanges

1 Carbohydrate   1 Fat
3 Very Lean Meat

Calories 234
   Calories from Fat . . 63
Total Fat . . . . 7 g
   Saturated Fat . . . . . . 1 g
Cholesterol . . . . 73 mg
Sodium . . . . 514 mg
   With 1 Tbsp
      soy sauce . . . . . . 214 mg
Carbohydrate . . . . . . 12 g
   Dietary Fiber . . . . . . 0 g
   Sugars . . . . 7 g
Protein . . . . 28 g

*I*ndex

ALPHABETICAL LIST OF RECIPES

About the American Diabetes Association

The American Diabetes Association is the nation's leading voluntary health organization supporting diabetes research, information, and advocacy. Founded in 1940, the Association provides services to communities across the country. Its mission is to prevent and cure diabetes and to improve the lives of all people affected by diabetes.

For more than 50 years, the American Diabetes Association has been the leading publisher of comprehensive diabetes information for people with diabetes and the health care professionals who treat them. Its huge library of practical and authoritative books for people with diabetes covers every aspect of self care — cooking and nutrition, fitness, weight control, medications, complications, emotional issues, and general self care. The Association also publishes books and medical treatment guides for physicians and other health care professionals.

Membership in the Association is available to health care professionals and people with diabetes and includes subscriptions to one or more of the Association's periodicals. People with diabetes receive *Diabetes Forecast*, the nation's leading health and wellness magazine for people with diabetes. Health care professionals receive one or more of the Association's five scientific and medical journals.

For more information, please call toll-free:

Questions about diabetes: 1-800-DIABETES
Membership, people with diabetes: 1-800-806-7801
Membership, health professionals: 1-800-232-3472
Free catalog of ADA books: 1-800-232-6733
Visit us on the Web: www.diabetes.org
Visit us at our Web bookstore: merchant.diabetes.org